PRAISE FOR

Buy the Change You Want to See

"In Jane's insightful and provocative book, she shares fresh perspective on ethical sourcing—showing us how we can tap into the global artisan industry to disrupt traditional manufacturing. She showcases little-known ways that the private sector has become an accelerator for change in developing economies. Read this book to be inspired and reminded of our individual and collective power to create change!"

—Michelle Nunn, President and CEO of CARE USA

"This book presents a truly big idea—using your buying power for good. It is also a window into a great entrepreneur's journey, as Jane Mosbacher Morris turns that insight into big change across sectors."

—Bill Drayton, CEO of Ashoka

"*Buy the Change You Want to See* opened my eyes to the power we have to contribute to causes we feel strongly about when we open up our wallets to purchase the necessities and extra goodies in our lives. An excellent blueprint for how to start the conversation to effect change."

—Halle Stanford, President of Television, The Jim Henson Company

"A marvelous and stimulating must-read. Jane connects rising suppliers in the developing world to global demand for ethically sourced products. Time to not only look at 'overlooked' populations, but to embrace their astounding potential."

—Christopher M. Schroeder, author of *Startup Rising*

BUY THE CHANGE YOU WANT TO SEE

Use Your Purchasing Power to Make the World a Better Place

JANE MOSBACHER MORRIS
with WENDY PARIS

TARCHER
AN IMPRINT OF PENGUIN RANDOM HOUSE
NEW YORK

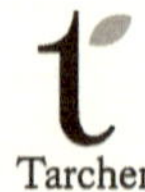

Tarcher
an imprint of Penguin Random House LLC
1745 Broadway, New York, NY 10019
penguinrandomhouse.com

Library of Congress Cataloging-in-Publication Data

Names: Mosbacher Morris, Jane, author. | Paris, Wendy (Journalist), author.
Title: Buy the change you want to see : use your purchasing power to make the world a better place / Jane Mosbacher Morris, Wendy Paris.
Description: New York : TarcherPerigee, 2019. | Includes bibliographical references.
Identifiers: LCCN 2018053136| ISBN 9798217185924 (paperback) |
ISBN 9780525504993 (ebook)
Subjects: LCSH: Business ethics. | Purchasing. | Consumption (Economics). |
BISAC: BUSINESS & ECONOMICS / Business Ethics. | POLITICAL SCIENCE / Political Process. / Political Advocacy. | SELF-HELP / Motivational & Inspirational.
Classification: LCC HF5387 .M877 2019 | DDC 658.7/2—dc23
LC record available at https://lccn.loc.gov/2018053136

Book design by Kristin del Rosario

The authorized representative in the EU for product safety and compliance is Penguin Random House Ireland, Morrison Chambers, 32 Nassau Street, Dublin D02 YH68, Ireland, https://eu-contact.penguin.ie.

155245421

For my husband,
Nate,
for inspiring me to pursue my vision relentlessly.

And for my parents,
Catherine and Rob,
for teaching me to value people equally.

CONTENTS

BUY THE CHANGE YOU WANT TO SEE

INTRODUCTION

WHY A BOOK ABOUT SOCIALLY CONSCIOUS CONSUMERISM? WHY NOW?

[Work] is about a search, too, for daily meaning as well as daily bread, for recognition as well as cash, for astonishment rather than torpor; in short, for a sort of life rather than a Monday through Friday sort of dying.

—LOUIS "STUDS" TERKEL, AUTHOR OF *WORKING: PEOPLE TALK ABOUT WHAT THEY DO ALL DAY AND HOW THEY FEEL ABOUT WHAT THEY DO*

In the spring of 2013, I found myself trekking down a narrow, poorly paved alley in the heart of bustling, chaotic Kolkata. I'd never been to India, but I thought I knew what to expect. I'd traveled pretty extensively, even to tough environments not set up for tourists, like Afghanistan. But I certainly *didn't* expect to meet a scrappy, young American working outside the largest red light district in Asia, and to begin reformulating my life's purpose in that place.

I went to India as part of my job with the McCain Institute for International Leadership, a new nonpartisan, nonprofit organization founded by Senator John McCain and his wife, Cindy McCain, a businesswoman and humanitarian. I'd just started at the institute and wanted to do well. It was just the two of us from our organization traveling together, Mrs. McCain and I.

We'd been invited by the International Justice Mission, a leading anti-trafficking nonprofit that works in India and around the world. We were scheduled to be in India for a week, traveling through red light districts and visiting aftercare facilities—safe houses where people get medical treatment, food, psychological support, and a place to sleep after exiting the sex trade. Many of them are girls—twelve-, thirteen-, or fourteen-year-olds who have been sold by their families into slavery, or kidnapped, or otherwise forced into prostitution. Aftercare facilities, often run with the support of an international or local nonprofit, are critical for helping survivors and also, ideally, protecting them against re-exploitation, such as from a trafficker who thinks he owns the girls working for him.

In many places, survivors of human trafficking are also at risk from their own families. In rare but heartbreaking occasions, a family member might resort to violence, throwing acid in the face of a girl who has been sexually exploited in an effort to reclaim the family's "honor," which they believe has been soiled by the girl's lack of "purity."

This book is about what I learned on that trip, which altered my life path and career. I saw in India not only survivors but also a real working model of something I'd long thought about—the private sector being harnessed to help address long-standing social problems. This book shares my story and the ways we all can help improve other people's lives through our purchasing power (without even changing careers).

So many of us want to help change the world yet feel overwhelmed by the problems we see. Contemporary media and technology bring home the world's struggles in a new and vivid way. We see images of Bangladeshi citizens walking through thigh-high water, and Syrian refugees washing up on the shores of Europe. Their plight is brought into our homes, yet we don't know how to help. We can feel just as powerless reading about tragedy in our own country. We may post about a cause on social media, but ultimately feel that we're not really making a difference.

It's easy to get "analysis paralysis" and to default to inaction. I can sometimes hardly read the news (and instead cheer myself up by looking at animals on Instagram). But what I've found is that the best way to take action is to remind myself of the tools that are at my disposal *right now* to make change. As I've grown older and developed a better understanding of my own sphere of influence, I see one clear way I can make a difference: harnessing my purchasing power for good.

Most of us don't realize how much purchasing power we have, and how much it matters. The average American family earns nearly $75,000 a year, and spends nearly $57,000. Half of that goes to housing, insurance, pensions, and health care, leaving nearly $30,000 for things like food, transportation, and non-necessities. That's a lot of money spent, daily, on things like coffee and groceries.

Our purchasing potential is like an untapped superpower. We might buy a morning bagel at one shop rather than at another because it's on our route to work, or drop thirty dollars on a gift card for a friend's birthday. But we can slow down and reflect on these micro-decisions, and make more thoughtful choices. For mom-and-pop stores in our country and micro-entrepreneurs in the artisan and agriculture sectors around the world, every purchase really matters. These businesses stay afloat because a handful of people or businesses decide each day to buy from them.

The artisan industry is the second-largest industry in the developing world, after agriculture. International trade in artisan-made products, what the United Nations calls "art and crafts," generates about $32 billion each year. Your birthday money, if spent on a bracelet made by a cooperative employing survivors of human trafficking, can have huge significance not just to the friend who receives it but also to the woman who rolled the beads for it. The money she earns selling bracelets could be what allows her to access clean drinking water or what pays school fees for her children. Our small purchases, when aggregated with those of others, can have a massive ripple effect. Our capacity to make change through purchasing is part of what makes me so excited about the conscious consumer movement, and what I want to share in this book.

I went to work at the McCain Institute after more than five years at the U.S. Department of State, working first on counterterrorism and later on human security, a catchall term for work addressing human trafficking, domestic violence, and sexual assault. I'd known I wanted to work in public service since high school. My grandparents had been in public service, as had my parents. My mother's father served in the U.S. Army, and my father's father worked in national politics. My mother started a nonprofit to help children who were in Child Protective Services in Houston and was later appointed to serve as the chairperson of the board of the Texas Department of Family and Protective Services. My father, in addition to his work in the private sector, also served in the government, focusing on national and international economic development and community well-being, throughout my childhood and to this day.

I grew up watching the dedication of my parents, and I felt passionate about carrying on a family tradition of public service. My parents definitely ingrained in me the belief that if I had an opportunity to serve others, I should take it—and they reminded me that opportunities to serve abound. My siblings and I each donated 10 percent of our allowance to nonprofits, but the real excitement in our house was about *doing*: going out as a family and serving a meal at a homeless shelter, or helping repair a house through Rebuilding Together, or ringing the bell for the Salvation Army at Christmas. (My dad still rings the bell every year.) In the United States, we have so much economic opportunity and freedom. I grew up with a strong awareness of this good fortune, and of the fact that we all have resources we can bring to assist others.

As an adult, I wanted to help improve the lives of those confronted by significant challenges. I was so grateful for the opportunity to work at the State Department. Yet during my time in government, I grew frustrated by the limitations of so many of our efforts to address humanitarian crises such as human trafficking, massive refugee migration, and real security concerns. Governments and nonprofits would step in with vital emergency assistance, but then be forced to walk away after the immediate crisis had passed due to funding constraints or a new catastrophe elsewhere.

The U.S. government donates millions of dollars overseas every year to help fund emergency housing, pro bono legal assistance, and medical and psychological services. These interventions are well-meaning and often critical. Yet again and again, as I saw, we come in with help during a crisis, then leave behind whole communities of people who have no real path toward reconstructing their lives. There are few jobs or chances of getting them. In most conflict and many post-conflict zones, the opportunity for dignified, stable employment simply doesn't exist.

The efforts I witnessed to help women in particular were almost always social service based rather than employment focused. Nor were women usually included in our counterterrorism efforts, as I learned during my tenure working on that issue. Counterterrorism efforts predominantly involved military and law enforcement training, and as in the United States, the security sector abroad is composed mostly of men. We weren't engaging half the world's population in fighting terrorism, an act that had almost become a social norm in some countries.

Women are the primary conveyors of social norms within the family, communicating behavioral expectations around things like substance usage and appropriate dressing. Why weren't we including them in the fight against terrorism?

While at the State Department, I helped craft a number of security programs focused on women's participation in combating terrorism. I eventually wrote the State Department's first Women and Counterterrorism Strategy, which laid out a variety of ways that the department could help bolster women's ability to speak and write against terrorism in communities where it was developing. The strategy also supported programming designed to help mothers have conversations with their children about not resorting to violence against civilians as a way to achieve political aims. The ultimate goal of including women was to have a more effective national security program overall.

I had the opportunity to travel around the globe to meet program managers implementing this strategy, as well as local women participating in it. I encountered a pervasive sense of powerlessness among many of the women I met. I was having lunch in Kabul with some women employed by the Ministry of Interior in Afghanistan, for example. These were among the most empowered women in the country, working in the capital city. Yet they said they were seriously limited in their ability to share their opinions, even at home, including about non-controversial topics like what they wanted for dinner.

I tried to understand the dynamics underlying their lack of personal agency—was it religion, culture, tradition? What I consistently came back to was one thing: money. Women in so many countries have little or no access to money of their own, whether earned, shared, or inherited. Even some women with jobs, like those I met in my travels for the State Department, weren't fully in control of their earnings once they got home.

Women's lack of access to capital and/or power over income meant they didn't fully make the decisions about their own lives in their own homes, let alone influence local and national affairs. They couldn't be part of peace talks and conflict resolution because their opinions were habitually, consistently dismissed—even about trivial issues. They had seriously limited leverage, which translated into almost no personal or social power.

After working on counterterrorism, I was detailed to the secretary of state's Office of Global Women's Issues to work on women's security. Here, I focused on domestic violence, sexual assault, and/or sex trafficking, in addition to national security. The office was led by a woman I admire deeply, Ambassador Melanne Verveer, whom I refer to as the fairy godmother of global women's empowerment. She could make things happen in a way that seemed almost magical. She was a true leader, and a true inspiration to me in terms of leadership. She also stood in stark contrast to the women I was meeting, who, once again, were vulnerable because of their economic insecurity. Poverty could lead to a woman being trafficked by her family. A woman's lack of economic power was also an absolute impediment to leaving an abusive home and protecting her children within it.

If a woman did get out of an abusive situation, she had few places to go and little way to support herself. Even if a woman was rescued or found her own way to escape, she was then stuck in the unequal power dynamic of the donor-to-recipient relationship. So many of the women I met were smart, capable, and hungry—not just for food but also for opportunity. They wanted to learn to read, in many cases, and to make a better life for themselves and for their children. But their lives had essentially been taken from them. Without a way to earn a living, they could not wrest back control.

When I was growing up, I had a strong sense of my own agency. There was a lot of conversation in my house about the value of work and of striving for one's personal best. In school, my brother, Peter, and sister, Meredith, both earned better grades than I did, and often with less effort. This became a major point of concern for me. I started to think I wasn't the "smart one" in the family. My parents immediately fought back against this developing negative self-image. They insisted that I *not* compare myself to others but only to myself. They would say, "You have to do the best *you* can do. That's all you can do." This idea of pushing for my best really stuck with me. There was a lot of fun and laughter in my house, too, but I definitely grew up with a huge amount of support for seeing the value of my contribution and believing that we all have something to give.

The lack of opportunity available to so many women directly clashed with my experience, and with my beliefs and values. I couldn't stand seeing their powerlessness, their lack of freedom. But what could they do to generate an income that would bring with it some autonomy? How could I help? I didn't have any specific plan in mind, or know what role I might play. But I knew I had to do *something*.

I decided to learn as much as I could about the process of job creation. I went back to school to get an MBA at Columbia Business School with this aim. I commuted to New York City from DC for graduate school for two years while continuing to expand the women and security programming at the State Department.

After I finished business school, I left the State Department to take the job at the McCain Institute for International Leadership. As my boss and co-workers knew, I was still figuring out what role I would ultimately play to help create sustainable change, ideally one based on employment.

MY "AHA!" MOMENT IN INDIA

From my first day in India, I experienced sensory overload. I'd catch a whiff of an amazing scent of curry cooking, breathe in deeply, then suddenly realize I was also inhaling the scent of burning trash or fecal matter. We'd see an incredible red sunset and the deepest green hills, then step onto a street next to pigs rooting around in a sewage stream. It was loud day and night. We passed beggars who had babies on their laps and plenty of people I felt certain were not getting enough to eat. There were social expectations about behaving in a proper, reserved way, but there were also adults defecating in the streets and families living in shanties so flimsy you couldn't fathom how they could offer real shelter.

Mrs. Cindy McCain and I were traveling with a small group from the International Justice Mission, driving around in a big, air-conditioned van with tinted windows, seeing the IJM's offices, walking red light districts, and visiting aftercare facilities. The traffic was so bad that we would inch along for two miles, the driver hitting the gas, then the brakes, then the gas, then the brakes. Families on mopeds buzzed by us. Sometimes the streets were too narrow for our van and we had to back up and try a different route. The roads were very uneven, the slab under one building butting up against the slab under the next. We were all clutching bottles of water, trying not to get carsick from all the stopping and starting. It could have been a great time to get to know one another, but it was hard to turn around to talk when the van was lurching around so much.

I had complete trust in our driver but less confidence that we wouldn't get stopped and harassed by thieves—or by officers of the law. Corrupt officials can be a part of the problem in places where human trafficking occurs. Some officials look the other way, take bribes that facilitate it, and, in rare cases, attack those who try to stop corruption. In 2016, a lawyer with the International Justice Mission was killed in Kenya while working on a case about police power. His client and driver were also murdered.

Because of the danger that trafficking survivors continue to face, aftercare facilities are generally unmarked, nondescript buildings—

sometimes right in a red light district, other times on the outskirts. We'd pull over on the main throughway, get out, and walk along the road past little markets and other cars. Then we'd cut across the street and into an alley, passing young women in cotton dresses and leggings sitting on dirty plastic chairs in front of shanties where they waited for customers. The shanties were basically three walls with a piece of metal for a roof, and a rope with a sheet hanging over the front as a door. Some of the girls played cards outside to pass the time, and men walked in and out of the curtained rooms, exiting carelessly, as though strolling out of a CVS.

We'd proceed to an aftercare facility. Inside, the leaders would give us a tour. They'd show us the kitchen and the sleeping room with its cots on a concrete floor, the curtains drawn. There would be generic posters featuring uplifting messages and drawings of rainbows, or maybe a stream, on the walls. Each shelter housed between one dozen and three dozen girls and women, and occasionally their children. The girls would often do a performance or show us artwork they'd made.

At one such facility we visited during the middle of our trip, we were sitting on the floor to watch a dance. There were ten or twelve survivors of human trafficking, in their teens and twenties, performing. Some looked like little girls, with dewy skin and silky pigtails. Others looked much older than their real age, trauma showing on their faces.

One of the young women had a son—an adorable, squirmy little boy who was three or maybe four. He was glomming on to me, squirreling around on my lap, trying to make my leggings snap against my shins. I zoned out for a moment, listening to the sounds of the traditional Indian guitar, holding this little boy. I found myself remembering the dance classes and performances of my own childhood. I'd always loved dancing and had grown up taking jazz, ballet, and tap. One time I'd dressed up as a raisin to dance to the song "I Heard It Through the Grapevine," by Marvin Gaye.

The little boy on my lap squirmed, jolting me back to the present, where I was sitting on the floor before a group of survivors of human trafficking. *What happens next for these girls?* I wondered. *And this little boy? After the dance, after the time at the shelter, where do they go? What do they do?* Once again, as at the State Department, I felt overwhelmed by the scale of the problem and frustrated by the limited options available. My mind was racing, trying to envision the next step for these girls.

And then, a few days later, we went to Sari Bari.

Our guide on the visit told us that we'd be seeing a social enterprise that was employing female survivors of human trafficking. I heard the words *social enterprise* and *employing*, but they didn't really register. I didn't fully recognize that we were now visiting a place altogether different.

We walked up two flights of concrete steps to a big open-air landing. There, we were greeted by an American woman named Sarah Lance, who introduced herself as the cofounder of Sari Bari. She didn't look much older than I am (although it turns out she has a full decade on me). She was immediately warm, with a big smile and freckles across her nose. She had a bright, sunny disposition and a youthful, disarming voice. She seemed to radiate a calm confidence.

We were standing just steps above a cracked blacktop road in a maze of a neighborhood, with its one-room brothels, goats tied to poles, and big-eyed, barefoot kids wandering around, clutching dolls or poking at random puddles. Sarah held herself calmly in the midst of this, and projected a different reality. She came across as strong, peaceful, and powerful. She seemed to me to be a kind of warrior; she had the energy you get when you are doing the work you feel called to do.

At that point, she'd lived in Kolkata for a decade, she told us.

She'd gone to India for the first time in her mid-twenties, after finishing her fine arts degree at California State Polytechnic and working a series of entry-level jobs. After that first visit to India, she wanted to return for a longer stay, and secured a position through a U.S.-based nonprofit to work at the Home for the Dying, started by Mother Teresa's Catholic order, Missionaries of Charity.

Shortly after she began working at the Home for the Dying, a male co-worker went out for a haircut. When he returned, he told Sarah that a young salon worker had offered him sex. She was working as a prostitute, a legal occupation in India, as she told him, to earn enough money to take care of her daughter and family.

That haircut changed the course of Sarah's life. She and her friend decided to learn more: Why were women like this driven to prostitution? Along with a handful of others, they began visiting the women in the largest red light district in India, buying them tea and listening to their stories. Sarah stayed on at the Home for the Dying for two years, while continuing to talk to the women in the red light district.

Many had been trafficked as teens, or even preteens, Sarah learned. They'd then been rejected by their families and had little or no exposure to life outside the red light district. As they aged into their mid-thirties, the only option for survival was to work as madams or traffickers themselves, exploiting other young women and taking part of their earnings. They were essentially trapped for life.

There were nonprofits working in the district that offered rescue services like the aftercare facilities we'd seen, but they focused largely on minors and rarely accepted older girls or women. Nor were there any groups offering real economic alternatives to the commercial sex trade. "What we heard was that they wanted an option out, and the route was through employment," Sarah said.

Sarah and her friends tried to think of a solution. Another volunteer at Missionaries of Charity, a woman named Kristin Keen, had the idea of starting a business selling *kantha* blankets. These blankets are a traditional Bengali handicraft of the poor, made from about five layers of old sari fabric. The women could sew these blankets, Keen suggested, and someone back home in the United States could sell them. Everyone loved the idea, and they spent six months looking for a nonprofit to start it. When no one came forward, Keen encouraged Sarah to start it herself.

Sarah agreed to try. A nonprofit immediately offered her a space to work and introduced her to three women who wanted to leave the sex trade and could be the first trainees. Through another nonprofit, Sarah found two sewing trainers, her first two employees.

The first year, they trained and employed three women. Sarah tweaked the model and today runs a program that grew out of it, composed of three months of part-time training, followed by three months of full-time training—both paid—and then full-time employment. Many women work in the sex trade while gradually making the transition out. It takes time, and often a lot of support, to make that change. Once employed by Sari Bari, women earn fair trade wages, plus benefits. Sari Bari pursues markets for their handicrafts.

At Sari Bari, Sarah outlined for us the simple business model she'd created to employ these survivors-turned-artisans. I peered through a concrete doorway into a workroom just visible past the landing where we stood. I was trying to process what I was seeing. About eight women were sitting on the floor sewing. The energy in the room was profoundly different from the atmosphere in the aftercare facilities we'd seen. In the middle of this chaotic neighborhood, Sari Bari felt like a peaceful haven where incredible work was being done, by women who would have faced an absolute void without it. There was a collective focus among the women in the room, a feeling that what they were doing mattered. The feeling I got from these women was *dignity*. The women were making money by doing good work, and their income allowed them to begin to take charge of their lives.

It's hard enough to start a business anywhere, but the idea that you could start a business in the middle of incredible suffering blew me away. It was a real working example of something I'd read about and dreamed about—the private sector being used to generate economic opportunity and economic development in communities that traditionally struggle. Here I was, seeing this happen in such an elegant way. I was totally taken by how straightforward the idea was: you serve a community by starting a business to employ the people in it.

Sarah invited our group to buy products on our way out. I was delighted to see how easy it was for people to spend money on these items. It wasn't a hard sell. It wasn't like trying to convince people to change their ways, like urging locals to purchase a cookstove that would eliminate the toxic particulates spewing from their traditional method of cooking over an open fire in the home. We were just buying beautiful bags and toiletry cases. I probably pick up three or four small bags in a year anyway. The items practically sold themselves.

What could be done with that? I asked myself. *How could I help Sari Bari and places like it?*

THE POWER OF THE PURSE

After that trip to India, I became obsessed with finding a way to link Sari Bari and similar co-ops to American consumers. I was on fire with the vision of making this happen. I thought about it all year, and then left the McCain Institute at the end of 2013 to work on it full-time.

When people hear the term *market-driven solution*, they often think that means relying on the free market *instead* of on government, or to the exclusion of regulations and nonprofits. I see government and nonprofits as crucial parts of economic and social development. But when it comes to long-term, sustainable, *economic* solutions to entrenched social problems, business is often a third, critical piece.

Retail is a massive force in the U.S. economy—a $2.6 trillion industry, two-thirds of our total gross domestic product (GDP). As such, retail purchases can be powerful tools for social change. Nonprofit giving and government aid are much smaller, about one-fifth the size of retail, in terms of dollars spent. Grants and government funding also can be fickle, and get cut too easily. Even the best aid efforts or interventions are vulnerable to what's in vogue in terms of the foreign policy priorities of the country administering them, or even the shifts in priorities of a foundation or nonprofit.

The market is fickle, too, but revenue-generating businesses have layers of oversight that are lacking in government aid programs, at least at this point. And the profit motive can force creative solutions for continuing to do business. In business, if a product becomes unfashionable, the company must find a way to keep operating, to pivot. A for-profit can't just walk away when interests change because it has too much money tied up in the equipment and staff, production facilities, and operations.

I love and have built a business around the idea that we can change the world for the better with our wallets. The purchasing power of individuals *and* of major companies can be harnessed for good and lead to concrete improvements in people's lives. The company I started, To the Market, economically empowers vulnerable communities around the world by hiring them to make the kinds of products you and I buy every day.

Since starting my business, I've seen both individuals and major corporations make real efforts to source from producers like Sari Bari, and to ensure that the groups they order products from are paying fair wages, employing at-risk communities, and/or using manufacturing processes that respect the environment. All of us buy so many items for personal use, and the companies and agencies we work for and run procure huge numbers of office materials, promotional products, and recruiting swag. We all can improve people's lives simply by changing where we buy our cup of morning coffee, our host or hostess gift, our team T-shirts, the centerpieces on the tables at our company's annual gala or dinner or award ceremony. We can pay attention to where our products come from, who made them, and how.

Another exciting truth about this moment in time is the scale of global production capacity, and the scope of the supply chain that it can feed into. Small groups offering fair trade and ethically sourced products are proliferating, and they are increasingly able to connect with huge numbers of buyers and multinational companies.

Still, even with all these good intentions and the great work being done, it's easy to dismiss conscious consumerism as trivial—how much good can one bracelet do?

A great deal, it turns out.

Purchasing ethically made goods helps generate sustainable income for real people, and that—combined with social support—can turn around lives. "I have seen profound transformations," says Sarah Lance of the women who work at Sari Bari. "There is no logical explanation for it, other than that human beings are resilient. If you give them an opportunity to rise above their circumstances, they will. These women are not beggars. They're not children. They're not the elderly. They are adult women who want to take care of their families."

It takes time, for sure. At Sari Bari, it takes about two years for most women who work there to move from survival mode to a more forward-looking mind-set. But Sari Bari gives them that time. "I have profound hope that they can have a whole life, be economically self-sufficient and relatively emotionally healthy," says Lance.

Our purchasing power can also provide real opportunity for future generations. Most women at Sari Bari have children, and through the group's social service arm, these kids get support to go to school and graduate high school. In 2018 alone, nearly sixty children participated in the school support program. Some of the women's children have gone through the program and enrolled in college—these are kids whose mothers had received, for the most part, little or no education. They couldn't read or even sign their own names when they arrived at Sari Bari. This is the power of economic opportunity, and we can help provide it.

As Lance puts it, "A business, if it works, can sustain itself. It's not that I think the world needs more purses necessarily. But it does need more economic opportunities for women. I believe in employment, in providing jobs and a way for people to take care of themselves."

Work—and the income earned from it—gives people the freedom to use their voice, to speak up for the changes they want and need to see made. Without earning power, others can silence you. Employment is not the immediate intervention needed in the moment of crisis, but it is the only way I have seen that allows individuals to move from recovery to real independence. Employment is a long-term, sustainable approach to empowering those in need. I want every person struggling for dignified work to find it, to have that spark in their eyes that I witnessed in Kolkata and to know that they are valued contributors to this world. Economic independence empowers.

In this book, we visit people who have lived through experiences that are hard to imagine. It's important to acknowledge the real suffering of others to help address their ongoing challenges. My intention in sharing these struggles is to inspire action through a means many of us have not fully grasped—the power of the purse to do good.

The book highlights cooperatives and businesses that offer ethical employment. It shares not only how the dignity of work affects real people but also how each of us has the power to make change through the supply chain. I recommend practical actions we all can take—as individual consumers, retailers, employees, or entrepreneurs—basically anyone empowered to make a purchasing decision.

The following six chapters look at some major categories of consumer and corporate spending—gift giving, customized goods, factory-made shoes and apparel, coffee, and chocolate—as well as recycling and the role of reuse in today's world. The chapters focus on products we wear and consume—the items that connect us viscerally and physically to the people who made them. I don't provide a list of "no-go" companies or materials; instead I highlight solutions that are working and companies striving to do good.

This book shares what I've learned from partnering with talented and capable artisans, farmers, and other skilled workers who have overcome incredibly difficult circumstances, and from working with businesses that prioritize social good. It's been an inspiring journey. I hope it inspires you, too.

CHAPTER ONE

WEAR YOUR VALUES

Custom Products That Reflect More Than Your Favorite Logo

In order to be irreplaceable one must always be different.

—COCO CHANEL, FASHION DESIGNER

On that first trip to India, when I visited Sari Bari with the McCain Institute, I also went to another extraordinary business, an artisan cooperative called Freeset. Operating just outside Sonagachi, the largest red light district in Kolkata, Freeset calls itself a "freedom business," a company that helps create freedom for those who have previously been exploited. Freeset's mission is to see the ten thousand prostituted women (and men) in its neighborhood liberated from the sex trade and free to do dignified work.

The artisans employed by Freeset upcycle sari fabric and sew custom jute and canvas bags, T-shirts, and key chains, which they screen-print with logos, quotes, and bold graphic images. Mrs. McCain and I went there with the team from the International Justice Mission, and when we arrived Freeset gave each of us a great navy travel tote. It had a cross-body strap and the phrase *Be Free* screen-printed on one side. I put my wallet and sunglasses in it, slung it over my body, and wore it the whole week (after I tied a red ribbon around one strap to make it feel more "me"). The ability to do custom screen printing differentiates Freeset from many other artisan groups. The jute bag was highly functional and so sturdy that I took it with me on another trip to India and Nepal a year later. But I had no idea at the time that the little bag would play such a key role in my future business.

Freeset's building looked huge and drab at first glance, a multi-story cement-block structure resembling a parking garage. But the color and activity inside were amazing. I stood in the central courtyard, looking up at just-washed, colorful sari fabric—manufacturing scraps, unsold yardage, and discarded garments—hanging from clotheslines strung between the balconies. The women there would transform these discards into beautiful new bags. I craned my neck to watch as several women in traditional dress, sitting on a floor high above me, carefully braided long strips of sari into handles and zipper pulls for cotton or jute bags.

Our whole group tramped from floor to floor, trying not to trip over one another as we navigated the narrow, steep stairs. There were workshops on every floor and storage rooms for heavy rolls of organic cotton. We stopped at the third level, and I peeked over the railing. I could see down to the ground floor, where two women sat on the chipped concrete floor next to a pile of fabric scraps in aqua, copper, mustard, and rose. One woman was leaning gracefully against a low wall, her legs stretched out before her, delicate ankles crossed, shiny black hair twisted into a low bun. She wore a white sari decorated with vibrant red and yellow flowers, the top draped over one shoulder, exposing a gold cotton-spandex shirt underneath.

The two women looked to be in their thirties or forties. I was struck by their calm focus and their elegance. Freeset employs many women in their thirties, forties, and fifties, giving them—like the fabric they sew—a second chance. It was an encouraging scene to witness, these two women working quietly together, transforming this traditional fabric into useful, appealing products. I smiled when I noticed that both women wore gold jewelry. Throughout many parts of the world, having enough money to buy a gold necklace or bracelet is a milestone, a signifier of financial stability. The fact that these women were sitting serenely in their beautiful dresses, working hard and wearing gold, indicated a level of economic security—and to me, spoke to the dignity that the opportunity to work afforded them.

Freeset was started by a New Zealand couple named Kerry and Annie Hilton. The Hiltons moved to Kolkata with their four children in 1999 with a vision of living among the world's poorest people. As they tell the story, they rented an apartment that looked fine during the day, only to discover at night that it happened to be located in the center of the city's largest red light area. Their new neighbors were the thousands of women forced into prostitution by trafficking and/or poverty.

The Hiltons, much like Sarah Lance, quickly realized that so many of the women yearned for an opportunity to earn money in some other way. They, too, got the idea of handicrafts. After experimenting with different products and testing the market, they decided to offer the women training in jute bag construction for the export market. They opened Freeset in 2001 with twenty women. Today, the two hundred plus workers can turn out one thousand bags a day, almost all of which are customized. They earn twice the going rate of other seamstresses in India and also receive health insurance and a pension plan, as well as health education, psychological support, and other social services. The products Freeset makes offer customers a consistent level of quality, a key to remaining a competitive, self-sustaining business.

The products were so well done that I wanted to take home more.

HUMAN TRAFFICKING
WHAT IT IS AND HOW TO FIGHT IT

Sonagachi, the most infamous red light district in Kolkata, is maybe a square mile, but Freeset estimates that more than ten thousand women live there, most working in the sex trade. The neighborhood is loud, dirty, and chaotic. Thousands of men visit daily. Many of the women in Sonagachi are from Bangladesh, Nepal, or rural India. Most have been trafficked—lured by false promises of good work or marriage—or even kidnapped or trafficked by a relative. For most, including mothers driven to prostitution to feed their children, poverty has left them without any clear alternative or way to leave.

The term *trafficking* basically means "to trade or exchange," and it's used to describe all kinds of illegal trade, including of drugs, weapons, and people. If human trafficking, the buying and selling of people, sounds like slavery, that's because it is. The International Labour Organization estimates that human trafficking is a $150 billion industry, and that an estimated forty million people are living in modern-day slavery in this way.

Both adults and children are trafficked for sex, hard labor, and warfare. Regarding sex for money, anyone under the age of eighteen is considered a victim of sex trafficking according to U.S. federal law, because it's happening below the age of legal consent. A runaway who winds up on the street, turning tricks to survive, is considered a victim of sex trafficking. Sexual exploitation has devastating consequences on children, including a higher risk of carrying infectious diseases, malnutrition, post-traumatic stress disorder, depression, and suicide.

Labor trafficking describes adults and children forced to do various types of work against their will. As with sex trafficking, victims are held through coercion, fraud, force, or the threat of force; they're often lured by false promises of decent work, then forced into inhumane conditions and hours, and prevented from leaving. They may be barely compensated and forced to pay a high recruitment fee, which places them in debt bondage. Traffickers often take their passports and money, and make threats against them or their families if they leave.

Child labor trafficking plagues many of the products we use today. The U.S. Department of Labor lists 136 goods made in 74 countries that are at significant risk of being made with child labor, including tobacco from Brazil and cotton from Burkina Faso.

The rate of forced child soldier recruitment has risen alongside ongoing conflicts in Africa and Asia. Children as young as eight have reportedly been used by the Taliban, Congolese, and South Sudanese militias in the last few years, while the Islamic State of Iraq and the Levant (ISIL) has developed targeted programs to forcibly recruit child soldiers, dubbed "cubs of the caliphate." This trafficking has also resulted in young men and some women fleeing their home countries out of fear of forced recruitment, leaving them alone and vulnerable to other kinds of exploitation such as labor and sex trafficking.

There are so many great organizations working to end human trafficking. A donation to any of these is an immediate way to fight back:

- CAST, the Coalition to Abolish Slavery, is a twenty-year-old group dedicated to ending trafficking in Los Angeles, one of the largest centers for human trafficking in the United States.

- ECPAT International uses a network of local civil society organizations in almost one hundred countries to help counter child sex tourism.

- Free the Slaves works locally in vulnerable communities, with programs that help impoverished Nepalis spot international traffickers posing as foreign labor recruiters.

- Freeset Trust teaches women in India skills that are necessary to truly experience freedom, including reading, writing, budgeting, and basic health care.
- Human Rights Watch does major advocacy work on behalf of child survivors and victims of forced labor, lobbying governments and the public to have zero tolerance for issues like children working in cotton fields.
- Humanity United works very closely with businesses to help fight labor trafficking, including investing in technologies that give more supply-chain transparency.
- International Justice Mission helps to eradicate trafficking through the justice system, operating as a kind of pro bono global law firm for the poor. They've helped free labor trafficking victims from brick kilns, quarries, and mines.
- The McCain Institute works on anti–sex trafficking legislation, as well as labor trafficking in agriculture, in partnership with the Howard G. Buffett Foundation. I sit on the McCain Institute's Human Trafficking Advisory Council, which includes leaders from the for-profit and nonprofit world.
- Polaris Project operates the United States' National Human Trafficking Hotline and has helped to set up other nations' human trafficking hotlines.
- Sari Bari USA is a U.S.-based nonprofit that helps fund the training, health services, HIV/AIDS support, and school program of Sari Bari India.
- Thorn, known as the Digital Defenders of Children, uses technology to deter predators, identify victims, and disrupt child sexual exploitation platforms.

I bought a pencil case and a few other bags printed with uplifting quotes, partly to support the co-op and partly because you never know when you need a gift. I didn't realize these bags, along with my new navy travel tote, would wind up serving as samples for my yet-to-be-envisioned company—or that customization would play such a huge role.

THE QUEST FOR INDIVIDUALITY IN OUR HYPER-CONNECTED WORLD

When I was growing up, we had small, personalized items commemorating special occasions around my house, and I always loved them. I had a round, silver jewelry box that my grandfather gave me when I was born, with my initials and birthdate engraved on the lid. I still have this box in my living room. My grandfather has since passed away, and seeing this box on my end table every day makes me think of him, and feels very special.

We also had inexpensive customized objects in the house, and these, too, felt meaningful. My brother and I shared a bathroom when we were kids, and my mom ordered each of us a set of bath towels with our first names (so we wouldn't fight over washcloths or bath sheets). His were red while mine were navy, both with white lettering. After my sister was born, she got in on the act (white towels, navy letters). It felt very sweet and homey to have my own towels, and I have continued to order the same style, from the Company Store, into adulthood.

Personalizing products—from monogramming towels to engraving the back of an engagement ring to customizing keepsakes—has a long tradition. In Western culture, the idea of carving initials to show ownership or origin dates back at least to ancient Greece. Greek coins often had the first one or two letters of a city engraved on one side, or the name of a ruler, and a profile on the other. The word *monogram*, in fact, comes from the Latin "mono," meaning "only," and the Greek "gram," meaning "unit." (You can see these early monograms at coin shows or in catalogs of rare coins.)

In the Middle Ages, merchants marked their goods with a type of monogram, or added a seal with their initials or other personal marks. These seals were a precursor of today's trademarks, a way of showing origin or uniqueness. Artisans, tradesmen, painters, and publishers also used initials to identify their works or their guild. The kind of personal monogram we tend to think about today really took off in Victorian England. The rise of a moneyed merchant class brought with it the desire among these newly rich to distinguish themselves, to appear upper class and refined. One popular way to assert status was by monogramming linens, lockets, shirts, and seals. A wealthy, non-noble family couldn't have a royal crest, but its members could display their family name or initials in ornate letters. Many of us grew up with these kinds of monogrammed articles around our homes, and we still give and receive them.

The desire for personalization has really intensified in recent years, certainly among my generation. A lot of my friends design sneakers for themselves on Vans.com, Newbalance.com, Adidas.com, or Nike.com. You can choose wacky color combinations and even add your initials or upload an image. I've ordered custom sunglasses for bachelorette parties, screen-printed T-shirts for church outings, and personalized birthday cakes for my husband, Nate (including one with Oscar the Grouch climbing from a garbage can, because Nate runs a waste and recycling company).

For my thirtieth birthday, my friend Natalie gave me a pair of

TOMS shoes that had been hand-painted with Disney princesses by someone she located on Etsy. She knows I love everything Disney—the parks, the movies, the company's story. To get these shoes made, she had to scout out my size, find an illustrator, and choose which Disney princesses to include. Her effort meant so much to me, and I love the fact that no one else has these shoes.

Not everyone wants Disney princess shoes, but we all use clothing and accessories to make a statement about ourselves. When I started looking around, I noticed my peers were personalizing all kinds of products, in new and novel ways. Some people give monogrammed journals and ties, cover their arms with tattoos of special words or images, or plaster stickers all over their MacBooks—all attempts to stand out and be unique.

Many people feel increasingly compelled to establish and assert their own personal brand, for a variety of reasons. I think we're seeing a huge uptick in customization because of this, and because it's increasingly difficult to make any kind of unique, personal statement through clothing bought off the rack. The Internet has made style more universal, and it's easier than ever for factories to quickly replicate a high-fashion garment at a low price with fast-to-market production.

Meanwhile, the expansion of international distribution routes by new and existing carriers has turned those living in formerly inaccessible nations into viable (and eager) purchasers. We have global style leaders, and anyone can copy them. That's always been the case somewhat, with ready-to-wear brands copying haute couture, but not to this degree, not as quickly, and not all around the world. (I read a hilarious op-ed by the investor Lawrence Lenihan in the *Business of Fashion* about the ever-shrinking time line of the fashion cycle. He notes the speed at which an on-trend item now goes from being introduced by a "cool kids" brand and selling at high-fashion stores to becoming the equivalent of "dad/mom jeans" sold at Kmart.)

WHAT "CUSTOM" MEANS NOW

There are so many ways to make something yours (or "theirs," in the case of a customized gift) beyond initials or a wacky design. You can buy the change you want to see by taking a broad view of the idea of customization. In the case of a gift, I really like including a note sharing why the business I bought from is special.

Choose How It's Made: You might buy from a company producing in a zero waste production facility or that specializes in low-environmental-impact production. You could choose to purchase products made by hand, for both the unique, personal feel and because you value artisanship. You might love fabrics that have been woven or dyed in a traditional technique, made by a community keeping that skill set alive. You could choose agricultural products like coffee or chocolate that are shade grown (rather than cultivated at a massive, clear-cut farm), or free-range chicken or beef.

Pick What It's Made Of: Your products might speak for you through their constituent parts. Vegetarian? You can buy on-trend "vegan leather" bags from small-batch maker Matt & Nat, or vegetarian leather from high-end label Stella McCartney. You might look for T-shirts made from recycled plastic bottles, scout out furniture and paper made from sustainable wood or fast-growing grasses, choose stemware made from recycled glass, or snag a party dress at a vintage store.

Decide Who Will Make It: You can customize a blouse or bag by buying one made by someone in a community you want to support, such as workers in the United States or in a specific union (look for union labels). You might want to support people with autism or a physical disability, and your customization could mean buying from companies employing those groups. If you're focused on criminal justice reform, you can buy from a prison program; for more than eighty years, the Maine State Prison Showroom has been selling amazing handcrafted wooden gifts made by inmates, including rocking horses, Adirondack-style chairs, and beautiful, intricate model sailboats. The nonprofit Fashion Revolution has started a campaign called #whomademyclothes, which allows workers and brands around the world to post pictures of their workers that are captioned "I made your bag."

Identify Your Ideal Seller: You can buy from companies that source ethically, or from local, independent grocery stores or food cooperatives. You might customize by shopping at a business started by a mom (or dad), or from a parent or neighbor trying direct selling through a company like Avon, Noonday Collection, or Sseko Designs. You might choose to support the entrepreneurial endeavors of an older adult or a recent grad. You might also focus on the give-back component: Does a potential seller donate a portion of proceeds to veterans, marine research, animals, or something else you care about?

All these factors mean that a company like the Gap can sell the same skirt in multiple nations, and that a shirt you buy at a store like JCPenney might show up halfway across the world, with some small change to the design, at a store selling it for a third of the price. In today's hyper-connected consumer environment, it feels like everything is everywhere.

I was in Asia in the summer of 2017, touring factories that produce apparel and shoes for the fashion conglomerate VF. (I'd recently begun serving on VF's Responsible Sourcing Advisory Council.) I saw seamstresses and shoemakers at a factory in Cambodia dressed in jeans and fitted T-shirts that could have come directly out of my own closet. To the Market also has a partner cooperative in Cambodia. There, I met with a young, upbeat co-op manager and jewelry maker wearing a ruffled denim miniskirt, espadrilles, and a black-and-white gingham shirt with two cotton lace ruffles down the front. I would wear any of those pieces, which she might have bought in any of the local boutiques in Phnom Penh. I'd felt the globalization of fashion but hadn't yet considered how it might help vulnerable communities.

I was also aware of a growing trend in customizing products through *how* we purchase them, not just what we buy—the basis of the conscious consumer movement. Recent Pew research on millennials found that members of this generation will pay more for eco-friendly products and that we believe our values are reflected in the brands we wear and carry. Ordering T-shirts screen-printed by at-risk youths in the United States, for example, feels like an increasingly relevant way to make an important statement about ourselves, to say that we care about others and that we want to make a positive impact. This rise in conscious consumerism was evident among my peers, and among businesses I'd studied in business school and those I'd read up on since.

Like individuals, companies are working harder than ever to stand out. Companies need to create positive brand associations, and to make their values clear to consumers. This effort really matters in today's increasingly crowded global marketplace, and in response to growing scrutiny from consumers, investors, and employees about business practices. Increasingly, companies are seeking to tell stories about themselves that show they are being "good citizens" in the world and that showcase their corporate social responsibility (CSR) efforts. In 2015, more than 80 percent of Fortune 500 companies published CSR reports, compared to only 20 percent just four years earlier—a sign of their focus.

Standing in the screen printing room of Freeset on that first trip, I had an immediate sense that its customization capability could be hugely marketable. I hadn't yet connected this capacity to the economic and social pressures on businesses, nor did I have my own company at the time; I'd just begun working for the McCain Institute. But I was aware of the increasing drive to say something unique about ourselves and our businesses. At that moment, the fact that Freeset could add a custom logo to a product made by a survivor of human trafficking felt like a double incentive for a potential buyer—and got my mind working.

When I returned from India, I couldn't get Freeset and Sari Bari out of my mind. I began thinking about how I could add value to the work they were doing. How could I create more opportunities for the women employed there? I knew their products were well made and could compete with those of traditional manufacturers. But their story was a hundred times more compelling—if people had a chance to hear it.

I started researching the artisan industry. I read about the economies and market dynamics dominating the developing world. I talked with founders of artisan businesses to better understand their struggles and the most promising directions. I thought about the future of consumer behavior, and researched the product categories that were currently selling well and the types of retail businesses that were flourishing.

I'd launched plenty of initiatives at the State Department and the McCain Institute, but I'd never started a business. I knew I had an affinity for creating new projects, and a comfort with tapping into my network to locate the people and resources needed to make them work. I'd spent a decade learning how to identify the decision makers within an organization and fine-tuning my natural skill at rousing enthusiasm for a new idea that challenges the status quo. I'd also grown accustomed to looking for people's personal motivations, and I largely accepted the reality that most people will support a new initiative or make real change in how they operate if they can see how it benefits them.

I bounced various business ideas off my friends and co-workers. I'd often show people the bags I'd brought back from Freeset and Sari Bari as a way to help illustrate the story and demonstrate the quality of their work.

I was thrilled to see how much people got it, and how easy it was to communicate my excitement about the founding and vision of these businesses. I knew I was onto something.

By the end of 2013, I had an initial outline of a business plan—at least the first iteration of it. I would connect with a couple dozen cooperatives employing vulnerable communities around the world, including Sari Bari and Freeset, and launch a website to sell their products to consumers here. None of these groups had an easy way to reach people in the United States. Even if they put up a website, they lacked the marketing budget necessary to help people find it. I'd do the promotion on the U.S. side and work to expand their market. I really believed there was a huge opportunity to increase the distribution of the two groups in India and others like them.

I made a few key decisions about my business structure right away. We would be for-profit. I felt strongly that if my message to vulnerable communities was about the dignity of work and the power of economic opportunity, my operation needed to be sustainable on its own and generate profits for itself, its employees, and its investors. Our social impact would come from *who* we employed and *how* they were employed, rather than through a give-back model. I was driven to start this company by my deep-seated belief in the transformational value of work—so evident on that first trip to India. All products we sold would be made by groups employing vulnerable communities in an ethical way. Our partners would be on the ground in these communities, paying a fair wage and offering safe working environments. I wanted a business model that would help vulnerable people to regain—or gain for the first time—their agency. I wanted to be a part of giving them choices.

In December 2013, I left the McCain Institute to get started. I spent the next nine months building up the back end of what would become To the Market's direct-to-consumer website. My goal was to launch the site in time for the holiday shopping season of 2014.

I had a huge amount of work to do, from building a website, to figuring out pricing, to creating a distribution system, to finding the ethical producers whose work we could sell. I put the word out to people I knew and trusted. I told them about the business and that I was looking for groups to represent, specifically those that employed survivors of human trafficking, sexual assault or domestic violence, ongoing conflict, natural disasters, or stigmatized diseases. I got referrals through friends and colleagues, and made time to visit or asked friends to visit these groups. People really went out of their way to share the news about my developing company, which felt incredibly encouraging. I was so passionate about this idea and about my personal role in helping create economic opportunity. I think others stepped forward to help in response to my heartfelt commitment.

WAIT! THERE'S A BUSINESS FOR THOSE BAGS?

We launched our consumer website in November 2014, as planned. Right away, something surprising happened; we began to get inquiries for custom goods from nonprofits and businesses. We had nothing on the site about custom orders, no subsection for corporations and nonprofits. But people reached out to request information about custom products for their organizations. They saw connections between their work and ours that I hadn't recognized—whether they worked for groups that supported women, fought trafficking, worked to end conflict, focused on international development, or promoted economic empowerment.

Corporate swag, it turns out, is a huge business, with more than $20 billion spent on it annually in the United States alone. The combined business expenditure on logoed products in the United States is more than the total economy of many countries, as I soon learned. I hadn't fully recognized the scope of the custom goods space at the business and nonprofit level. I'd worked in the public sector for most of my career; there's not much room for swag in the government. Sure, the State Department's Office of the Chief of Protocol would occasionally order messaged giveaway items, but the government doesn't have a major marketing arm, and there are important regulations around gift giving to avoid the appearance (and reality) of favoritism or bribery. Businesses and nonprofits, however, have a huge need—and often a serious budget—for logoed products that promote their brand and tell a positive story about their work and their values.

My first order came *before* I'd even launched the site, from the McCain Institute, which focuses, in part, on fighting human trafficking in the supply chain. A former colleague needed two hundred bags for a conference and loved the little jute travel tote I'd shown her from Freeset. She thought it would be great to purchase bags like those, screen-printed with the conference logo. These would be bags whose very creation supported the McCain Institute's anti–human trafficking mission.

Immediately after I launched the site, the mother of my friend

Kelly, who is involved in the University of Texas's Center for Women in Law, connected me with their conference organizer. She thought that, given the center's focus on women, it would make sense to have bags made by women for that year's annual convention. These, too, were screen-printed. Then an order came in from Humanity United, a large private funder of anti–human trafficking work in the United States. They wanted custom screen-printed tote bags to give to members of the Alliance to End Slavery and Trafficking (ATEST).

Once I launched my company, this happened again and again. Despite our online focus on direct-to-consumer accessories (and our truly minimal outreach to promote custom goods), there was ongoing interest from people working at organizations who saw connections between our work and their mission, or our vision and their customers' interests, or our producers and their stated CSR aims. Some requests came from employees who had taken that next step in their thinking about swag, realizing that the products that bear their organization's name could, and should, reflect the values they espouse. Even small- and medium-size businesses buy branded merchandise, participate in marketing events and recruitment fairs, and order client gifts and orders came from them, too.

Businesses today need to show that they are doing good in the world, and to focus like never before on branding. Businesses are facing what I have come to call a "trifecta of pressure and interest" that didn't exist as recently as ten years ago. The first part of this trifecta is growing consumer demand to know more about how the products they buy are made, particularly among millennial and Gen-Z shoppers (but also among Gen Xers and even some baby boomers). We don't trust large corporations as much as people did in the past. We're skeptical, questioning, detached. Technology and the mass communication that has come with it have made us more aware of the importance of safe working conditions and a fair wage; we're far less comfortable buying goods that may have been produced in unsafe or inhumane ways. As consumers today, we ask ourselves: *What had to happen at the factory for this shirt to cost only two dollars?* Companies are increasingly being challenged to answer these kinds of questions.

Investors are also demanding answers. In the past couple of years, showing good corporate citizenship has become increasingly important because a growing number of socially conscious investors are screening potential investees through a lens of environmental, social, and/or governance standards, often called "ESG." These kinds of considerations are becoming serious factors in billion-dollar-plus investment decisions. Pension funds, for example, are shying away from companies with poor ESG, such as those that dump hazardous waste or buy from dangerous factories.

The second part of the trifecta is increased scrutiny by the press, investors, employees, and amateur investigative reporters. Companies can't really operate in a black box of secrecy when it comes to sourcing anymore because people are asking questions, sharing information, and applying pressure on retailers to make a positive impact on the world.

New regulations are the third part of the trifecta. The California Transparency in Supply Chains Act, which went into effect in 2012, requires retailers and manufacturers that do business in California and have worldwide gross receipts of more than $100 million to report on their websites their actions to eradicate slavery and human trafficking in their supply chains. As the state's resource guide on the act puts it, "An estimated 21 million people—11.4 million women and girls and 9.5 million men and boys—are victims of forced labor around the globe." California, which boasts one of the country's largest consumer bases, has a unique ability to make demands on business. But Californians are not alone in using information about sourcing practices to make purchasing decisions; as a recent survey of Western consumers revealed, many people would be willing to pay extra for products they could identify as being made under good working conditions.

In Europe, the United Kingdom's Modern Slavery Act of 2015 is designed to tackle slavery in England and Wales. Companies cited for slavery, human trafficking, and exploitation can have their assets confiscated and be required to make reparations. As James Brokenshire, then the Parliamentary Under Secretary for Crime and Security, put it, the act will "send the strongest possible message to criminals that if you are involved in this disgusting trade in human beings, you will be arrested, you will be prosecuted, and you will be locked up."

It's so important for CSR (and ESG) objectives to be sustainable. Sadly, if there's no clear business case for them, those programs can be the first to get cut if sales are down, leaving that charity or group in the lurch. Companies have begun to recognize that they need not only to have viable social good goals, but also to ensure their continuity. One of the best ways to guarantee a social initiative's survival is to tie it to the core business interests, which logoed merchandise clearly can do. If a company buys bags from Freeset, a type of purchase it is going to make anyway, it can say to the world, "Look at our social responsibility. We support women-owned businesses and source products made by vulnerable communities with 100 percent organic cotton."

Not all corporations are looking for ethically produced swag, but I think they should. This money has already been allocated; it's just a question of changing where it's spent. If your company focuses on the environment, and then hands out plastic key chains that people immediately toss, there's a disconnect between your mission and your method that undermines the authenticity of your message. If people throw out that key chain or magnetic calendar (with your business logo on it), they're figuratively trashing your company and literally making you contribute to the proliferation of waste. Customizing in a way that aligns with your company's values, on the other hand, gives a far better return on investment. It's also easier, and often less expensive, than you may realize. If you think about your organization's marketing goals and CSR objectives, then consider the variety of techniques that can be used to decorate so many different things, ideas will come to you—as I was seeing. People at every level of an organization have power to harness the market to make change in this way. You may be in charge of a small, regular purchase at your company—such as speaker gifts or office supplies—and that decision-making power can have a big impact on someone else's life.

HELPING A BIG BANK MAKE A BIG DIFFERENCE

At the end of 2016, a friend connected me to someone who worked as a vice president in marketing and events at the Manhattan headquarters of Union Bank of Switzerland (UBS). The banking industry struck me as the perfect partner for To the Market. Banks host numerous large-scale events, tend to want upmarket gifts for attendees, and usually have fairly progressive corporate social responsibility goals. Also, the quantitative focus of a banking industry event can be pretty dry; a gift with an uplifting story would be a welcome addition to a day-long meeting or statistics-heavy conference. A bag sewn by the women at a cooperative like Freeset would also let the bank create a more personal connection with attendees and share its social values.

101 CLASSIC CUSTOMIZATION
PUT YOUR STAMP ON IT, LITERALLY

While the ways in which we customize have expanded, many of the techniques and materials used to add monograms or logos remain the same. Here are some options.

Screen Printing: Each individual screen allows a different color of ink to seep through onto a material, adding up to one beautiful image. The more colors an image has, the more individual screens have to be created, and the more expensive it becomes. This is the most popular customization option for To the Market's clients for bags and T-shirts because of its vivid colors and durability.

Heat Transfer: Similar to screen printing but less expensive, this method of transferring an image or logo from one material to another works well for vinyl tablecloths (think trade show coverings) and cotton bags. Heat transfer requires high temperature and high pressure and allows for complicated images, like a photograph, to be transferred to hundreds of pieces—though that heat-transferred picture on the back of your T-shirt may not last through repeated washings as well as a screen-printed one would.

Embossing: Great for adding a name to a set of thank-you cards or a logo to a leather-bound journal, embossing is a high-end, understated way of personalizing by creating a raised image on the material, without additional color. Debossing is basically the same idea in reverse: a recessed relief image.

Embroidery: The art of writing with thread, embroidery is an elegant way to add your name, initials, or logo to fabric. Embroiderers use colorful silk or cotton floss, or even gold or silver thread, and write in a variety of stitch styles. The backstitch creates one long line, as with a pen, while the satin stitch fills in a large area with color. This traditional craft your grandmother might have enjoyed is often done by a machine today. If you buy a pair of Mickey Mouse ears at Disneyland or Disney World, you can watch the embroidery machine add your name to the back while you wait (I happen to know.)

Engraving: While I think of silver as the classic material on which to add a monogram, plenty of companies engrave glass, wood, or even stationery. Engraving means cutting a design into a hard surface, from initials into a tree with a pocketknife to a logo onto a glass with a laser engraving machine. Early printing was basically engraving; the text or image would be cut into a plate, which was inked, then pressed against paper.

Giclée: If you've seen those personalized prints on canvas of your friends' kids or dogs that look like they were painted, you've seen a giclée print—basically a high-quality inkjet print done on canvas. The creation of super-high-quality printers, often using archival-quality ink, has allowed for these one-of-a-kind art-quality prints.

Wax Seal Stamps: A wax seal—melted wax that is stamped with a metal, wood, or cork die, then hardened—once served as an authenticator, much like a signature today. Mentions of wax seals can be found in the Old Testament. This method of signing a document fell out of favor as literacy, and the ability to recognize a signature, became more widespread. Today, wax seals are a sophisticated addition, used to close an envelope elegantly, or as a decorative embellishment on paper, wine bottles, or ribbon.

On a chilly Wednesday in December, I took the train from Washington, DC, to New York. The UBS building is in the heart of Midtown, a soaring black glass tower near Radio City Music Hall, connected to the underground shops and restaurants of Rockefeller Center. The building itself feels like a branding statement. The huge floral arrangements on the receptionist's desk, the solicitous security guards, the key card to enter the elevator banks—all these things say: this company is successful and elite; it recruits and retains the best talent, it's a best-in-class organization. Just entering the building reminds you of your value. The lobby seems to proclaim, "You're in an important place. You matter!"

These huge corporate headquarters can also feel, well, *corporate*—massive and impersonal, with cubicle after cubicle on floor after floor. This feeling made me more even excited to share our story, because one individual employee at a place like UBS can make a procurement decision that touches real people in a real way. I felt sure employees would welcome a chance to do something outside the ordinary at work.

I checked in at the desk, and the woman I was meeting, Letitia, came down to get me. We sat together in her cubicle, and I explained that I saw an opportunity for UBS to showcase its values through the products it already buys. I explained how making even small changes in the supply chain, such as by procuring ethically produced swag, would be a great, easy, visible way to promote the company's social responsibility objectives. Businesses have largely been in autopilot about swag, but UBS *could* spend money on customer recruitment in a way that reminds potential customers, investors, and employees of its values. I articulated my vision to UBS.

I got the order immediately. It was for thousands of screen-printed bags for conferences throughout the coming year, which would mean thousands of dollars to Freeset. The bags would be high-end, made of 100 percent Global Organic Textile Standard (GOTS)–certified cotton. They would be lined and zippered, have three pockets, and be printed with the UBS logo. That one decision by Letitia and her team was incredibly valuable to Freeset. The order helped the artisans pay rent, send their babies to the on-site day care, and provide schooling for their older children. This order, and others like it, continue to help break the cycle of poverty, which can otherwise persist for generations.

The order gave me a huge shot of confidence. It was exactly the kind of proof of concept you look for when starting a business or pivoting to a new line. For me, it was a sign that even massive companies can source differently. We can disrupt the supply chain (as so many in the agricultural space are already doing). The scale of possibility at corporations was thrilling.

During our first two years in business, my business model began to shift more and more toward disrupting the supply chain of multinational corporations. It became increasingly clear to me that the custom goods market could play a far larger role than I'd originally planned.

The idea of starting lean—as in, not investing too much in a certain product or direction until you get feedback from the market—was really ingrained in me during business school. We were taught to put out a minimally viable product to potential customers and then pivot based on their feedback. I was glad to have this mind-set, which enabled me to seize upon the interest at the corporate level. This could be the *real* opportunity for these ethical producers, I realized, and for my company.

UBS presented the first batch of bags to executives attending a consumer retail conference on March 8, 2017, which coincided with

International Women's Day. The conference was at the Four Seasons Hotel in Boston, and UBS invited me to attend, and displayed a big vertical poster about To the Market in one of the networking areas, near the food, where attendees hung out. I was so encouraged by their desire to highlight our work and their own corporate responsibility efforts.

Later, one of the women from the marketing department told me that non-executive attendees were asking about the bags. Where could they get them? This validated the idea that we can change how we purchase supplies. People were so excited by the quality and the story that they went out of their way to inquire about carrying a bag with *someone else's logo* on it.

WEAR YOUR VALUES 2.0

I had a business, I had orders, and I'd recognized a whole vein of potential customers to tap. Now I had to see if I could get more orders from big corporations—including those where I hadn't personally worked or didn't have a friend of a friend, or know someone's mother.

In the beginning, I was ordering all the custom tote bags from Freeset. But our partners around the world were working in all kinds of materials and making so many things. Couldn't other groups do custom corporate products? How could we match what they made with the needs of companies? Unusual items that probably had never appeared in a corporate context began to seem possible, and relevant—and special. Take an oil and gas company like Shell. Wouldn't holiday ornaments made from upcycled oil drums (by one of our our partners in Haiti) be a more compelling investor or employee gift than, say, a phone charger that might well break within days (as happened on a great

HOMEBOY INDUSTRIES IN LOS ANGELES

Homeboy Industries sits on one of the most forlorn corners of downtown Los Angeles, a concrete patch near Chinatown, facing a silent school bus depot and a section of the elevated train. Muscle-bound men pass in and out of the front doors and stand in groups on the sidewalk, most in T-shirts or tanks that display the tattoos circling their arms and rising over their shoulders, marching up their necks, and stretching across their shaved heads. Yet there's a feeling of safety on this corner, an invisible bubble of peace that can only be explained by the work being done and the power of the person who started it. Homeboy Industries is one of the largest, most comprehensive, and most successful gang intervention, rehabilitation, and reentry programs in the world.

Thirty years ago, Father Gregory Boyle, an ordained Jesuit priest, began serving the men and women in the poorest parish in the Los Angeles archdiocese. This was in the mid-eighties, when gang violence exploded across East LA. Father Greg (as he likes to be called) realized that young people in his parish needed a viable alternative to gang life, and came up with a novel approach: offering compassion and a job. This grew into Homeboy Industries as it is today, complete with psychotherapy and weekly math and reading sessions, drug and gang members anonymous, classes in parenting skills, anger management, domestic violence prevention, and meditation—all part of a comprehensive eighteen-month program designed to heal individuals from the inside out. The philosophy is simple but rarely seen put into action so effectively: a therapeutic environment and supportive community trumps a gang—and helps people envision a way out of violence, addiction, and incarceration.

The free tattoo-removal clinic also helps people start over. Tattoos can put a person's life in danger if they signify the wrong gang.

They might indicate that a person has been trafficked. They can turn off a potential employer in an instant. On average, more than a thousand people—both trainees and members of the broader community—head here each month to sit for the painful treatment. Doctors zap at the marks of an earlier life with a laser. It takes repeated sessions to break down the ink into small enough particles for a person's body to metabolize it.

The services are expensive, and Homeboy Industries is able to absorb the cost thanks to grants, donations, volunteer medical professionals, and nine social enterprises that generate about 30 percent of the organization's annual revenue and employ nearly three hundred people each year. Screen printing and catering are the most successful of its businesses, but they all provide training for future employment, either here or elsewhere.

To a customer, what also stands out about these enterprises is the quality of the products they produce. Take the tacos. The on-site Homegirl Café serves farm-to-table Latin-inspired fare from a take-out counter and a large, comfortable sit-down restaurant.

On a typical weekday it's busy, but not so crowded that you can't get a seat. Four LAPD cops in full uniform drop by for lunch, waving to one of the cooks visible behind the curved half wall separating the open kitchen from the diners. The cops settle in at a table with the air of regulars placing their usual order. They're as muscle-bound as the trainees. It's not hard to imagine these same officers of the law running into the waiters or cooks under very different circumstances. In here, they're all part of the same vision of rehabilitation through support and training.

If you sign up for a tour, one of the trainees will give it to you—perhaps Mark*, who has tattoos down his neck, including one that says "R.I.P." in big, black letters. Mark is thin and energetic, springy

*name changed

as Tigger. To start the tour, he stands outside on the sidewalk and points up at a huge mural of a butterfly painted on the concrete wall. The words *tenderness, freedom, hope,* and *love* are written in lilac and sky blue on the wings.

As Mark gestures at the mural, he tries to explain why he loves Homeboy Industries. Father Greg sees your value, he says, something that no one did, as far as he could tell, from the time he was born. Mark came here after spending eleven years in jail, finally getting out, and then finding himself bounced back in for a domestic violence incident. "That's all I saw growing up," he says. "Then I saw on the back of a T-shirt, 'You are exactly what God intended when he created you.'"

The idea behind that message—that he was intended, not a mistake, that he had worth—completely flipped him out and transformed his worldview. It made him come to Homeboy Industries and stay.

Mark knows everyone in the building and jokes with them in English and Spanish. While touring the classrooms on the second floor, he stops at a bulletin board with a list of grades of fellow trainees now attending college. He points to an A gleefully. "It's like it's contagious, seeing someone get an A in history," he says. "One of us, from our circumstances, got an A. It's so inspiring."

Later, back out on the street, Father Gregory Boyle arrives. He swings past the restaurant in his loose gait. He's wearing baggy khakis and has a thick, white, neatly trimmed beard and a round, smiling face. Father Greg is far younger looking than you'd expect for someone who has such a huge presence in the city, and who has made such a big impact on the lives of so many of Los Angeles's most marginalized communities. No one is beyond hope to Father Greg, as the title of his best-selling first book suggests: *Tattoos on the Heart: The Power of Boundless Compassion.*

In Homeboy Industries' screen-printing facility, trainees learn to create silk-screened custom logos and images for corporations, schools, nonprofits, churches, and government. You can get a quote online or buy various logoed items at the on-site store. As when buying from Freeset, wearing a shirt or carrying a bag customized by the men and women at Homeboy Industries makes a statement about your belief in the power of personal transformation. Each order also helps ensure that the programs and services remain free.

Today, Homeboy Industries is helping other groups in other cities replicate their model of support, training, and earning for marginalized populations, including the homeless, people with mental health problems, and those in addiction and recovery.

Portlandia episode)? The opportunities suddenly felt boundless. There was so much room for creativity, for our partners and for To the Market.

Almost as soon as I began thinking about these kinds of product extensions, I began to get orders. The American Red Cross, a group that has done a great deal of work in Haiti, ordered wineglass charms made from upcycled paper from an artisan group we work with in that country. Mastercard's Center for Inclusive Growth, which focuses on moving people from poverty to prosperity, placed multiple orders for corporate gifts for high-visibility events such as the World Economic Forum. These gifts reflected their brand identity and advanced their core mission of sustainable economic empowerment. Today, we've expanded our custom ethical supplier base to more than one hundred partners in over twenty countries, and most can make products for businesses. It's become the core focus of our company, far bigger than direct to consumer. It's also the track that is making our company stand out. Working with corporations means larger orders, making it a better financial model for us, and more lucrative for our producers. We increasingly distribute orders for our most popular items to a handful of cooperatives to provide steady work for many—rather than subjecting one producer to a surge in orders, followed by a fallow period, forcing it to lay off workers.

We're continuing to develop a sales strategy that will let us act as a matchmaker between the capabilities of ethical producers and the mission and needs of various companies. Shifting the business this way has allowed me to think differently about artisanship, workers, and materials. I try to find the compelling attribute about a product that makes it a great fit for a corporate or nonprofit client.

I was at a female founder retreat sponsored by a law firm I use and love (and have turned into a customer), Fenwick & West. I was talking to another attendee, Kara Goldin, the founder and CEO of the San Francisco–based company Hint, which makes unsweetened flavored water and has an environmentally progressive ethos. Goldin asked if we could make our market tote bags in a fabric created from 100 percent recycled plastic bottles. Hint sells water in fully recyclable PET plastic bottles, and it made sense to have bags fabricated from the same material. I was delighted with this request. I'd just connected with a supplier of fabric made from 100 percent recycled plastic bottles. It's a great new product, and learning about it had already started me thinking of ideas for companies that use plastic in packaging or in their core product. This is another level of customization we offer, the fabric itself.

It's exciting to see how we can expand our impact by piecing together the different narratives and asking these questions: Who made it? How is it made? What is it made of? All these things are additional layers of customization. I think this is where consumer and corporate products are going.

We're also switching our own marketing materials to 100 percent recycled products. To the Market is constantly going deeper in terms of aligning our own business to our mission. As the ethical fashion nonprofit Remake says, "Wear Your Values."

CHAPTER TWO

THIS BRACELET BUILDS COMMUNITY

Gifts That Give Back

Giving—and thoughtful, generous giving at that—may be more rewarding than receiving on numerous levels, from the neural, to the personal, to the social.

—MARIA KONNIKOVA, AMERICAN AUTHOR

On a cold, rainy Monday morning in November, I drove from Washington, DC, to New York City with six huge duffel bags of products in the back of my car. They were for To the Market's first-ever Macy's in-store event, a trunk show at Macy's Herald Square, being held just in time for the holiday gift rush. I was carrying items I thought would make great gifts—holiday ornaments created from discarded oil drums by impoverished artisans in Haiti, table runners and placemats made from upcycled saris by survivors of human trafficking in India, necklaces and bracelets created by refugees living in Greece, and beaded jewelry and clutches made by refugees in Uganda. I had no idea how much people would buy, so I erred on the side of bringing more than I might need. I loaded it all in my ten-year-old gold Acura MDX that I'd inherited from my mother and drove to my friend LeAnne's in Harlem, where I was staying for the week.

My company had been up and running for two years by then. We had steady business-to-business relationships and a growing revenue stream.

Still, I knew that an important part of our company was missing—partnerships with major retailers. I wanted to help change the supply chain of the retail industry, too, and selling our products at stores alongside those made in traditional factories would be an important step.

I'd worked for a year to get into Macy's in hopes of becoming a regular supplier. Everyone in retail considers Macy's a whale—a huge victory to land. Practically every designer and clothing and accessory manufacturer sends samples. Macy's is such a big retailer that landing the account can make a huge difference for a company's bottom line. For a small company like mine, having Macy's as a partner also would ease negotiations with other stores. If we could reliably fulfill a purchase order for one of the world's largest retailers, that would give other corporations more confidence in our ability to meet their own procurement needs.

Tuesday morning, I headed downtown from Harlem to Macy's. It was still raining and even colder, but as I neared the store, I felt excited. I'd gotten this far in my effort to land an account from the legendary retailer.

We were doing our trunk show on Giving Tuesday, the Tuesday after Thanksgiving. Black Friday and Cyber Monday are the two largest shopping days in the United States, but many people are still looking for holiday gifts on Tuesday. The average American spends almost $1,000 a year on holiday presents. Giving Tuesday, founded in 2012 by the 92nd Street Y in New York City and the United Nations Foundation, is designed to encourage people to think about humanitarian giving and ways to help those in need. The day felt like the perfect time to talk about To the Market and the power we all have to change lives by giving gifts made by vulnerable communities.

One of my favorite stories about meaningful gift giving is O. Henry's "The Gift of the Magi." A poor husband who owns almost nothing beyond a pocket watch decides to pawn this single treasure to buy his wife a Christmas present—a fancy clasp for her lustrous hair. She, meanwhile, secretly chops off her hair and sells it in order to buy a chain for his pocket watch. Christmas arrives. The big reveal. Oh no! He has no watch for the chain, and she no hair for the clasp! They realize, through these gifts, how much they already have—lives rich in love.

This tale has warmed hearts for generations, and it highlights an experience we've all had: feeling cared for by receiving a gift, far beyond the value of the object itself. There's an art and a value to receiving, too. Accepting gifts gives others a chance to feel generous and caring. In "The Gift of the Magi," the sacrifice these two lovers make for each other also points to this aspect of giving—how much joy it brings to the giver. As Harvard psychologist Ellen J. Langer has noted, refusing a present prevents someone else from experiencing the joy of giving. "You do people a disservice by not giving them the gift of giving," she has said.

I love giving gifts. It's an easy way to let people know you're thinking about them, especially when you choose something that has real meaning for the receiver (Disney princess shoes!). I actually have an annual gift budget—that's how important this aspect of social life is to me. It's also part of why Christmas is my favorite holiday. I appreciate the meaning and spirit of it, and the decorations and being near family. But I also love the presents.

IT'S BEGINNING TO LOOK A LOT LIKE CHRISTMAS

Even from the outside, Macy's Herald Square felt magical, with its holiday decorations and lines of people standing outside to get a glimpse of the Christmas window displays. Inside, huge diamond-like solitaire ornaments hung from the ceiling, along with long strands of glass droplets that looked like giant icicles from a fairy-tale Christmas. It felt very *Miracle on 34th Street*, one of my favorite holiday movies. Macy's Herald Square is the iconic urban department store, a National Historic Landmark covering an entire city block in Manhattan. It's nine stories high, and is one of the largest physical retailers in the world. The escalators on the upper floors still have their original wide, wooden treads (that your heels fall through, if you're wearing pumps). They creak upward like an old wooden roller coaster, passing racks of fabulous clothes and housewares—and at that time of year, evergreen wreaths and boughs and sparkling lights and ornaments. I was excited to be there not only because Christmas is my favorite time of the year, but also because if sales went well that day, Macy's would likely place an order to carry our products for spring.

It turns out that gifting is its own retail category, like accessories or housewares. I love the fact that retailers recognize the important role of gift giving in society. The gift market is an estimated $130 billion plus each year, with promotional or corporate gifts accounting about 20 percent of that. This is an encouraging figure to me, considering the number of products we sell that are bought as gifts.

Helping me with the sale that day was a part-time teammate based in New York named Mary. Macy's had given us a small alcove space on the mezzanine, overlooking the main floor, maybe two hundred square feet of space. I could gaze past the railing and see the entire ceiling of the first floor below us flickering and glowing. Shoppers rushed around, bundled in scarves and hats, fur hoods and mittens, hijabs and hoodies. They carried big white Macy's shopping bags printed with the word *Believe* in red. They spoke Chinese and Arabic and French, the languages blending together in an energetic, expectant holiday buzz. Snippets of conversation float by in that kind of crowd. "My God, why can't we stay in here all day?!" Or, "Can you take a photo of us? We just got here from Florida this morning. It was eighty-four degrees when we left!"

Our stall had held an Etsy shop before us and would go on to hold a Michael Kors scarf display the next month. On this day, it was only us. We set up our stuff by ten a.m., and I didn't leave that spot all day (other than to run to the bathroom). Much to my delight, I realized we were situated right next to a Starbucks. Anyone taking a break to buy a latte or plopping down on the coffee shop's leather ottomans for a rest could look through the wire mesh wall separating the spaces and see our goods. This was a fabulous location because we had incredible foot traffic, and (almost as compelling to me) we could see the coffee. I drink a huge amount of coffee. When I'm traveling (which I am 90 percent of the time these days), I practically have coffee on an IV drip.

Starbucks is one of my favorite coffee companies because of its leadership in making high-quality coffee a staple for so many, and in using its purchasing power to improve farmers' output and incomes. Even as the company has expanded, Starbucks has stuck to its principle of purchasing fairly grown coffee, developing its own certification program for growers, called C.A.F.E. (Coffee and Farmer Equity), which is similar to fair trade. (To learn more about Starbucks's role in transforming the coffee industry, see chapter 3.) The company also offers employees health insurance. Nearly every coffee company worth its sugar has a fair trade line today, or some other way of assuring consumers that the farmers who grew the beans were decently paid. This is exactly what I hope to see in retail—using our mass love of fashion for good just as Starbucks uses our love of coffee for good.

Mary was doing shuttle runs throughout the day for caffeine and egg-white-and-turkey-bacon breakfast sandwiches (both of which I like to consume at all hours of the day). The rain drove shoppers indoors, and people were spending serious time looking. For twelve hours, I stood there drinking coffee, sharing our story, and helping people identify the right gift for each person on their list. "You're shopping for your mother-in-law? How about these great upcycled horn spice bowls?" I'd say. I don't get tired when I'm evangelizing about our products. I delight in sharing with people how they're made, who made them, and the value of gifts that give back. Most important, I relish the chance to explain why I believe in the products' ability to change people's lives. Artisans such as those working in cooperatives in Uganda, Greece, and Haiti feel the impact of our purchases immediately and profoundly on the ground.

I talked about how buying a bracelet made by a mother in Uganda helps pay for her children's school fees. (School is not free in so many parts of the world, and a lack of access to basic education generally means the next generation lives in the same poverty as the current one.) I talked about the usefulness of the little animal-print toiletry bags made by Freeset, how they help survivors of human trafficking build independent lives, and how the bags are just the right price for Secret Santa gifts. I showed off our Ethical Totes, amazingly useful, splurge-worthy large black bags with wide caramel-colored straps made from discarded goat leather by artisans who have survived ongoing natural disasters in Haiti. I showed the gold leaf cuffs, also from Haiti (I'd designed myself!), and rattled off potential gift recipients. "Girlfriend? Sister? Boss?" Shoppers would pick up the cuffs, push up the sleeves of their coats, and try them on.

I was very aware that this day was a significant moment in the arc of our business, the first time we were being shown by a retailer the scale of Macy's. It was one of those moments when you just know that you are experiencing something very important in your life (and hopefully in the lives of others). I had worked hard to get us in there, which felt satisfying in itself. But the real question remained: How much appetite would there be for gifts that give back among customers of Macy's, shoppers at a huge retailer focused on mass appeal? I knew the products spoke for themselves in terms of quality and design, but would the story help generate enough sales for Macy's to place an order for spring?

BRINGING ETHICAL GIFTS TO A RETAIL GIANT

My first "in" with Macy's came at a creative conference (one of my favorites—Alt Summit) in Salt Lake City in 2015. Macy's was one of the sponsors of the event. I met some people from the regional marketing department and talked to them about our company. I knew Macy's had an appetite for socially conscious purchasing because of the Heart of Haiti initiative the company launched after the 2010 earthquake that devastated that country. When it comes to positive social impact purchasing, one challenge for big, traditional companies, however, is figuring out how to incorporate it regularly into their business practices. A lot of companies have a corporate social responsibility division, but the buyers aren't in that division. There can even be tension between the CSR people, who are judged by social-impact metrics, and those in more traditional functions, who are evaluated primarily on financial performance.

Also, most major corporations aren't set up to work with nontraditional suppliers, such as an artisan group based in a remote valley outside of Port-au-Prince, Haiti. Procurement is a specialized skill set, particularly when sourcing from co-ops in undeveloped parts of the world, employing survivors who are in the process of learning new skills. A company like mine is a bridge between small-batch producers and major companies. We bring design and management support to the local producers and source from a variety of cooperatives, which lets us supply at the scale that a big company like Macy's needs.

I stayed in touch with the marketing folks from Macy's after the conference and later set up a meeting at their regional office in Houston. I flew to Houston to explain why we think consumers are interested in social-impact gift giving, and which items would likely perform well in their stores. I also stressed the fact that it's becoming increasingly important for stores like Macy's to source ethically because of the trifecta of pressure and interest from consumers, investors, and regulations. Sourcing ethically is no longer just a way to "get bonus points" with customers; rather, it's increasingly required by law and expected by consumers and investors.

That meeting with the regional Macy's team in Houston was encouraging but ultimately didn't lead to a next step. A few months later, I noticed on LinkedIn that a close friend from college, Kevin, knew a buyer who worked at Macy's in New York. I asked Kevin to connect me. I'm always looking on LinkedIn to see who I know, and then following up on introductions. Many people can be reluctant to ask for help, and to follow up. They worry about coming across as pushy or aggressive. But LinkedIn's core purpose is networking, and it's possible to be assertive and still quite considerate. You definitely don't want your focus on your goals to feel transactional to others. When people connect you, they're extending political capital, and it's always a good policy to let them know how much it means to you. I almost always write a thank-you note to someone who makes a connection for me. I'm a huge fan of asking for what you need and also taking the time to show people how much you genuinely value their effort, such as by sending a thank-you note or even a little gift.

SEND A THANK-YOU NOTE OTHERS WILL THANK YOU FOR

It's important to acknowledge the efforts that others make for us, whether they involve time, money, attention, or an introduction. Saying thank you is a small gesture that makes other people feel good, and has a major "return on investment" from a relationship perspective. Also, as research from the field of positive psychology shows, writing a gratitude letter to someone who had a special impact on your life, and reading it to that person, brings more happiness than fun activities like going to the movies. We get pleasure from giving. Here's how to express thanks and give back.

Choose Cards That Protect People or the Planet: There are so many beautifully designed cards made from recycled paper today; it takes almost no extra effort to send a note on one of them. Look for cards made from 100 percent post-consumer waste (PCW) paper. Or choose thank-you cards made from Forest Stewardship Council–certified wood (FSC) that comes from a responsibly managed forest and can be recycled. Bamboo is a sustainable fiber that can be made into super-luxe paper. Another good option is St. Jude Children's Research Hospital stationery, with incredibly cute pictures drawn by patients. Profits after expenses help fund the hospital.

Give Good Chocolate: So many chocolate makers and ethical candy creators have sprung up in cities around the nation in the past ten years. It's easier than ever to say thanks with chocolates that support a local maker, improve lives of farmers, protect important ecosystems, and promote sustainable growing. (See chapter 6 for suggestions.)

Send Sustainable Flowers: Who doesn't love a bouquet of flowers as an expression of thanks? The Bouqs Company works with farmers who use sustainable, eco-friendly growing methods, and only cut what they sell, avoiding wasted flowers. Or you can save money and support a local florist by logging on to Bloomnation.com, a community marketplace that cuts out the wire-service middleman and their fee. BloomNation lets you search for and order from a local florist, and view photos of that company's actual arrangements (rather than a stock image of a bouquet that may not match what you buy).

Kevin connected me to his buyer friend, Heather, in New York, and I took *another* flight to pitch my gifts-that-give-back vision, this time to the New York headquarters of Macy's at Herald Square.

Heather totally got it. She genuinely believed in what we were doing and felt that there was a strong place for us in Macy's. She introduced me to someone else, an omni-gift buyer named Sarah, who oversaw all sorts of gifting sections. This was the fourth person I pitched to at Macy's. Sarah and Heather became our champions. Since Macy's had already ordered everything they'd be selling for holiday 2016, they came up with the idea of doing an in-store trunk show on a consignment model.

Trunk shows are one strategy businesses are using to deal with consumer over-choice. Trunk shows can drive people into stores and attract the attention of overwhelmed consumers facing endless options for gifts and other products today.

On Giving Tuesday, we had that great location, but in some ways, we were lucky that shoppers found us at all, given how many other points of sale existed. There were nine floors of retail, and that was just within Macy's. If you looked out the windows of the Starbucks next to us, you'd see a Sephora on the other side of Thirty-Fourth Street, alongside Old Navy, Foot Locker, a luggage and camera store,

Skechers, and a now-shuttered, family-owned women's clothing store with its original sign still intact: "Cliquer's Colors Fashion Inc." An even larger sign hung above it: "Retail Space for Lease."

The Cliquer's storefront is a sign of the times for so much in the retail landscape. All these options existed on just one block in Manhattan. The Internet makes every home as competitive a retail environment as Thirty-Fourth Street. Because of this, retailers are looking for new ways to stand out and remain relevant.

Differentiation is a huge part of retail competition. During the last five years in particular, *price differentiation*—going cheaper than your competitors—has heated up, particularly online. People will generally buy a commoditized product, whether it's milk or a Nintendo game console, where it's least expensive. But competing on pricing alone is tricky and getting harder all the time. There is a race to the bottom, price-wise, and from a business and humanitarian perspective, everybody loses.

Another route to differentiation is to offer products that no one else has. This desire to sell something different has spurred the growth of private label clothing—pieces or collections that a company like Macy's buys from a factory or designs itself to sell under its own label, often adding a unique embellishment or signature style. Today, private label clothing, taken together, is larger than any single brand.

A third major way to differentiate products is to find things that have a good story and to share that story on the label or the website—particularly if it includes an element that makes people feel good about buying and giving. The quest for a good story combined with the need to offer items no one else has is where ethical sourcing comes in, and is great news for those of us who care about how our products are made. I'm optimistic that today's hyper-competitive retail environment, along with increased scrutiny and consumer pressure for supply-chain transparency, will continue to make retailers scramble for products made by artisans and other nontraditional makers around the world.

On Giving Tuesday, I'd brought six duffel bags of gifts that shoppers in New York couldn't find anywhere else, each with a great story. That combination is largely why we were able to get into Macy's. Now all that remained was seeing how well our gifts would sell.

RISING FROM THE RUBBLE—HAITI'S CREATIVE FORCE

I designed the gold leaf cuff I was selling at Macy's during my first-ever trip to Haiti, in the spring of 2016, about six months before the Macy's in-store event. I'd been invited by the Artisan Business Network (ABN), a business development group created through funding from the Clinton Bush Haiti Fund after the 2010 earthquake.

Although I first conceived of To the Market after being inspired in India, people face hardships all around the world. Haiti, for example, has been plagued by natural disasters and ongoing political and economic instability. I wanted to help harness purchasing power to support artisans in places like Haiti, too.

Haiti is about as far from the sparkly, perfume-scented sales floor of Macy's as one can imagine. An undeveloped, lush Caribbean country the size of Maryland, Haiti occupies the western third of the island of Hispaniola. The Dominican Republic covers the eastern side of the island, and while many people know the D.R. as a tourist destination with white-sand beaches and a bustling nightlife, Haiti is better known for tragedy and poverty.

Hispaniola is so mountainous that its original inhabitants, the

Arawak (who lived there when Christopher Columbus made landfall in 1492) called it "land of the mountains"; the name "Haiti" derives from the original Arawak word for this description. Spain claimed the island as its own before ceding the western portion, which now comprises Haiti, to the French. By the 1700s, the Europeans were calling Haiti the "Jewel of the Antilles" because it was the most successful of the French colonies, with its output of agricultural products including sugar and tobacco from plantations worked by slaves.

The slaves revolted in 1791, eventually forming the world's first independent black republic. They named it Haiti after the Arawak name. But the African slaves' hard-won independence was soon followed by internal conflict among leaders of the new country, as well as crippling trade embargoes by European nations. There was then fighting with the nation next door, a series of dictatorships, bankruptcy, and international interventions (including humanitarian aid) that often created nearly as many problems as they intended to solve.

Today, Haiti is the poorest nation in the Western hemisphere. It's so close to the United States, about 675 miles from Miami—roughly the same distance as between Miami and Atlanta, or Dallas and Denver. When you arrive, the crowds of impoverished people standing outside the gates of the airport and hanging around the little towns, clamoring to help with your luggage or wash the windows of your car in hopes of a tip, are a jarring contrast to the shiny cleanliness, soaring ceilings, and well-stocked stores of the U.S. airport you just left. Haiti has the lowest Human Development Index in the Americas, a composite statistic including life expectancy, education, and income per capita. This is the figure that the United Nations uses to determine if a country is considered developed, developing, or underdeveloped. As of the 2015 Human Development Index report, Haiti was ranked 163 out the 180 countries. (The United States is number eight.) More than half of Haiti's ten million citizens live in poverty.

If you look at the toll of natural disasters alone, it almost seems as if Haiti sits on the doomed side of the island. In 2004, Hurricane Jeanne hit Haiti, killing more than 2,400 people. Four years later, a series of hurricanes and tropical storms swept through Haiti, destroying infrastructure, knocking down power lines, and strafing roads in the capital city of Port-au-Prince.

Then in January 2010, a magnitude-7.0 earthquake struck just southwest of Port-au-Prince. This was the largest quake on the island in two hundred years. The earthquake killed about 200,000 people—some buried under rubble and never found—and left millions homeless.

The quake also destroyed many of the remaining grand nineteenth-century public structures in Port-au-Prince, including the parliament building, the main post office, the city hall, and the Notre Dame Cathedral. It smashed the United Nations building and killed 30 percent of the country's civil servants. Then Secretary of State Hillary Clinton is reported to have responded, after hearing about the earthquake, "Why Haiti?" Having seen so many impoverished parts of the world, she, like so many, just couldn't believe another tragedy would hit this nation.

While Haitians were still digging themselves out, there was an outbreak of cholera, introduced, it was later discovered, by a United Nations envoy there to help survivors of the earthquake. Cholera infected about 700,000 people.

After the earthquake, the artisans were a group that really needed help. They'd lost their workshops but not their ability to produce. As *New Yorker* writer Jon Lee Anderson put it in a 2016 article, one good thing came out of this really horrific earthquake: "The disaster drew the world's attention to Haiti's long struggle—and, to some extent, offered a chance for a fresh start."

This fresh start included the creation of the Artisan Business Network, the group that invited me down. The ABN opened an office in Port-au-Prince, and hired a director, Nathalie Tancrede. Tancrede is a Haitian American who was working in New York when the earthquake struck. She looked on Facebook for ways to volunteer, offered to help translate, and wound up moving to Haiti and taking the job running the new ABN.

I've met so many people like Tancrede since starting my business. Many are Americans, often missionaries, but I've also met leaders from Europe and other countries, as well as from within local communities. These are people absolutely dedicated to connecting struggling artisans with markets in the developed world. They are real heroes. It is unbelievably inspiring to travel to some of these countries with ongoing social and economic problems, and to meet the people making a difference.

Though the Clinton Bush Haiti Fund has closed down in the years since the earthquake, the Artisan Business Network got a grant from the Inter-American Development Bank, a multilateral financial institution focused on the economic prosperity of the Americas. The grant enabled the ABN to invite me and five other buyers and buying consultants to fly to the island and meet the artisans in person on a guided buying trip. The ABN also brings designers and consultants to the island, and even to the studios of artisans located in the very remote, mountainous interior. The global market changes quickly, and designers and consultants can help artisans choose colors and focus on products that are in demand at the moment, helping them mix their traditional craft with modern design.

I was thrilled to be invited on this buying trip to meet the artisans and see what they could do. Being on the island allowed me to see how the products are made and to connect emotionally with the artisans, which was the aim of our hosts. The trip directly helped me with product development, immediately expanding our ability to source from Haiti. I didn't have a network there, and Haiti is not a country I would necessarily be able to navigate by myself, making the guide immensely helpful.

The ABN is a great example of an effective development effort that includes the private sector. By bringing over companies like mine, the nonprofit ABN helped expand the marketplace for local makers. The trip connected artisans personally to private industry, essentially working to help citizens of Haiti pull themselves out of poverty through self-employment. This kind of public-private partnership brings together the strengths of for-profits, nonprofits, and government agencies to address serious social problems—and create potentially *sustainable* solutions, which I loved to see.

Sustainability is key. Many U.S. companies hurried down to Haiti to buy handicrafts in the aftermath of the earthquake. They ordered novelty items, often designed to be sold as gifts, aimed at generating immediate income for artisans. This rush of orders was a great help, but the projects weren't necessarily conceived of with a thought to the future. While in Haiti, I heard so many stories of designers or companies flying down to do a new "made-in-Haiti" collection. A co-op would hire a bunch of workers to fill the order. Everyone would get busy cranking out great products and bringing home cash to help them rebuild. But then the work on that collection would end, and the store or designer wouldn't place another order. The artisans had to be let go. Many didn't understand what had happened. Why was their work no longer needed? Wasn't it good? They faced a sudden return to unemployment or underemployment—and yet another instance of instability and dismissal.

I don't blame the designers; they're not development experts, and these interventions came from the right place and provided economic relief in the short term. But when it comes to making lasting change that lifts people out of recurring desperation, we need to think about the sustainability of our efforts and of those we choose to support. Just as rescue can be only a stopgap measure, so too can job creation. We have to evolve in how we operate in undeveloped countries, because what we've been doing for decades hasn't fully worked. Sustainability for the medium and long term has to be part of the metric we use to gauge success. If we create a job that ends in three months—or if we place a big order and then never hire the artisans again—we haven't solved the problem in any lasting way.

Economic consistency is part of having control over your life, whether you live in Haiti or in the United States. At my company, if we get a large order from a place like Macy's, we'll try to parcel it out to different co-ops in order to create opportunities for more artisans and to avoid the surge-and-crash scenario for any one group. Our model of sourcing from multiple cooperatives also benefits our business and helps with our own sustainability. By not relying on one specific group to fill an important order, we mitigate our own risk of failing to deliver.

When my group arrived in Haiti, the ABN's Nathalie Tancrede met us at the airport. We drove directly to see Caribbean Craft, the largest handicraft producer on the island and an expansive operation, as far as artisan cooperatives go. Nearly 150 artisans were hard at work when we arrived. They were scattered about in a handful of buildings, creating and painting papier-mâché home decor items, such as cute roosters, rhinos, and giraffes that could hang in a kid's bedroom or make a fun gift for an animal lover of any age, and adorable standing ducks. They were beautifully painted in bold colors. Caribbean Craft also houses one of TOMS shoes' painting facilities, where Haitian artisans create a special, limited line of hand-painted shoes.

Caribbean Craft is run by Magalie Noel Dresse, an energetic, upbeat young woman who was a real stabilizing force after the earthquake. She had enough purchase orders to continue employing people, even when other folks couldn't. (Oprah visited her after the earthquake.) I was impressed by the sheer scale of the operation, and the fact that they were making ornaments and wall art for West Elm, a highly successful retailer that has publicly committed to sourcing the majority of its products from ethical producers by 2020. Dresse won an Innovative Social Sustainability Bravo Award from the Latin Trade Group in 2013 for her work. Still, as people's memory of the earthquake began to recede, purchase orders were dwindling even at this well-established producer.

That night, we stayed at the Marriott hotel, a new, modern hotel whose very presence felt quite significant. A major international chain hotel suggests that a country is open for international business. It symbolizes business potential; there's a recognizable place to stay with the amenities a businessperson expects. I was aware of the importance of an international chain hotel from the U.S. government's efforts to get a large hotelier to open in Kabul. The government provided incentives to encourage this investment in Afghanistan with the idea that a good hotel would help spur more business development.

When we arrived at the Marriott, I was excited to see chandeliers, wall art, soap, and glasswork made by the country's artisans. Tancrede walked us around and told us which co-op or artist did what. It was a beautiful manifestation of how the local art and design could fit seamlessly into a high-end environment, and it made me excited about bringing products back to the United States to sell. The hotel also sold artisan products in a tiny gift shop that was about the size of a closet (a nice walk-in closet).

The next day, we drove to a workshop called Atelier Calla, run by Haitian designer Christelle Paul, who is well respected on the island for her design and business savvy. Paul has a very upmarket, sophisticated eye. I'd seen pictures of her work and was particularly interested in the fact that she was creating sleek, stylish items out of discarded cow horn from the island.

Atelier Calla was in a neighborhood that used to be quite nice but had recently been overrun by gangs. We arrived to find a concrete wall surrounding the compound, with a heavy sliding metal gate cut into it. We called out to the guard inside, who opened the gate, then shut it behind us. (This is a pretty typical setup in Haiti and other places in the developing world.)

Inside the compound gates, a half-dozen workers sat on metal stools in the courtyard, polishing small pieces of cow bone on their laps. Others wrangled large cow horns into buffing machines. It was hard work, but the atmosphere was calm. I could hear the workers chatting to each other above the whir of the buffing machine.

Christelle Paul stood just outside her office, wearing black, arty-looking glasses and a necklace she'd designed herself made from a leather rope and wooden pendant. She had a regal look, with her hair pulled back in one of those flawless, slicked-back ponytails, and a lovely, confident, contented smile. She showed us around the atelier and explained her process. Some of the artists were making little catchall bowls out of the polished horn, and I immediately knew they would appeal to U.S. customers. These became part of the collection we brought to sell at Macy's.

After leaving Atelier Calla, we drove to an inspiring operation called Papillon, focused on orphan prevention. Papillon employs impoverished parents who might otherwise give away children they can't feed (a surprisingly common practice in Haiti, as I learned). The two hundred plus parent-artisans at Papillon were busy making all kinds of amazing objects out of discarded materials, including beads rolled from old cardboard soda cases and strung into bracelets. A few young men and women, wearing jeans and T-shirts, with woven friendship bracelets wrapped around their wrists, sat at old wooden tables slicing up cardboard cases with paper cutters. They collected the resulting ribbons into long, neat piles. I could hear the *swish* of the blades coming down, and the conversation and laughter of the workers.

In the next room, other people rolled the strips into multicolored, disk-shaped beads and stacked them on long sticks, like lollipops of every hue. The printing on the boxes created a dappled effect, and the lacquer both fused the beads together and gave them a high gloss. They looked like pricey ceramic or glass beads. The creative atmosphere was infectious and I suddenly had inspiration for a potential corporate gift. Couldn't the marketing department of a consumer food company like General Mills, say, give social media influencers jewelry made from cut-up cereal boxes fashioned into similar beads? I snapped some photos to use in a pitch, and we continued on.

We left Port-au-Prince and headed inland toward Croix-des-Bouquets, a village about twenty minutes north of the capital. Almost all of Haiti's legendary metalwork, *fer decoupage*, is made in Croix-des-Bouquets. The metalwork tradition started in the 1960s with one Haitian artisan, Georges Liautaud, whose story is another example of the power of the individual to make change. Liautaud created flat, elaborate crosses out of old railroad ties to decorate the mausoleums at a local cemetery. Cemeteries in Haiti can be surprisingly ornamental, and Liautaud worked with themes of spirituality and magic, images of animals and local flora, and African and European symbols.

A local art dealer saw his crosses and commissioned him to make home decor. Artisans in Croix-des-Bouquets started imitating his style and technique. Soon a new kind of folk art was born, with artisans making bowls, candle holders, and various kinds of wall decor from upcycled metal, not just railroad ties but also the huge drums used to ship oil and, later, ketchup and soap. Liautaud's studio became the center of the new movement. The Art Institute of Chicago, the Museum of Modern Art, and France's Musée National d'Art Moderne have collected Liautaud's work, and museums have also collected metalwork of other Haitian artists.

As we approached Croix-des-Bouquets, I could see artisans sitting in small, pavilion-like workshops in their front yards, each with a roof and three walls, open to the street. I could hear the banging of metal coming from the front yard of practically every house. I couldn't wait to see what people were making. I jumped out of the car and walked ahead of everybody, popping into one stall and then another, eager to see the work. Entire families were running home-based ateliers, hammering old oil barrels into flat sheets, cleaning, chiseling, forging, cutting, polishing, and painting.

I saw so much activity around me. My wheels began to turn. I thought, *I'd like to take a bit of this and a bit of that!* Artists were applying gold leaf to a few items, and I thought it would look great on a piece of jewelry. Others were carving a leaf pattern onto wall art, and I wanted to see that on a bracelet, too. I would never pretend in a million years to be a jewelry designer, but walking through the village, I suddenly got a very specific idea for a bracelet I wanted to see. I asked the second or third group I met if they could make the design I envisioned. The artisans were open to the concept and seemed eager to give it a try.

Some of the artisans there were shipping as many as ten thousand pieces a year to New York City and Europe, I learned. One of the town's top artisans, Serge Jolimeau, sells his wares at a market in Santa Fe, New Mexico, every year. Jolimeau makes hand-cut metal wall art featuring fish, flowers, and Haitian women walking through jungles of palm fronds, their own hair flowing like vines. The last survey done by the Artisan Business Network showed that the Croix-des-Bouquets community had collective sales of more than $2 million a year.

It's exciting to see people around the world really appreciate the artistry of Haiti, but it's not enough. The artisans in Croix-des-Bouquets, for the most part, live pretty humble lives. Most people have their own homes, usually cement block structures without indoor plumbing. Life here is easier than in some of the rural parts of Haiti, where a family might live in a mud dugout, but people are still constantly hustling to pay for things most of us take for granted—like water. Everyone has to buy water in Haiti. Some areas have city water, but it only comes on once or twice a week. In rural areas and villages like Croix-des-Bouquets, they don't even have that. Several companies sell water, driving around with water trucks. You fill your tank at home or you can buy it for about one dollar a bucket. Most artisans buy it by the bucket to supplement cisterns they've set up to catch rain. Families need several buckets of water a day.

Since the Clinton Bush Haiti Fund closed down in 2015, the ABN has been searching for ways to stay afloat. The grant from the Inter-American Development Bank helped, as did one from the W. K. Kellogg Foundation. But when I visited, the IADB grant was coming to an end, and despite the success of a handful of artisans, the vast majority didn't have the sales connections yet to survive on their own. Getting grants to support artisan entrepreneurship can be tough, as many potential funders don't see the impact as clearly as they would if they were funding hospitals or roads. With artisanship, sales numbers and jobs created and sustained are the measures of effectiveness, and these can take several years to manifest.

During our trip, we visited many workshops in small towns, rural areas, and the city. It's hard to fathom the level of devastation caused by the earthquake and the ongoing poverty of the country. But Haiti also has an unbelievable artisan tradition, amazingly resilient people, and an entrepreneurial spirit that I found truly inspiring. The country is one of the top handicraft producers in the Caribbean, even wholesaling products to other islands.

There are a lot of explanations for why Haiti has such a thriving creative culture. Tancrede said she thinks that the Haitians' mixed African and European ancestry has created an exciting blend of cultural traditions that leads to inventiveness. I think the national ethos of creativity and entrepreneurship has built on itself and continues to generate its own momentum. And a lack of traditional resources can encourage people to find new ways to use old things; scarcity can be a driver of creativity.

Or maybe it's the land itself. Even the original inhabitants were creative. Christopher Columbus was apparently impressed by the woodwork and weaving of the Arawak on the island. He brought back some of their work, and it "stimulated the first real interest in anthropology in Europe," according to Eleanor Ingalls Christensen, author of *The Art of Haiti*. I definitely found myself caught up in the creative fervor and inspired by the feeling that you can make something unique out of just about anything.

For the last two nights of our trip, we moved to a beautiful hotel called Hotel Montana, made up of a series of small buildings scattered across a hillside high above the city. We could see the entire city laid out beyond the patio, and the clouds topping the mountains in the distance. The rooms were simple but cheery—painted bright orange and yellow, and outfitted with lovely fabrics made on the island.

Hotel Montana is known for its panoramic views, and for having been totally flattened in the earthquake. Before the earthquake, it had been a popular place for international visitors. (Brad Pitt was one of the hotel's celeb guests.) The quake destroyed the hotel, killing fifty-two people on-site. The owner was buried under the hotel during the earthquake and trapped there for a few days. The story goes that when rescuers finally unburied her, she stood up, brushed herself off, and said, "What took you so long?" Then she got right to work rebuilding her hotel.

To me, this story reflects the spirit of the country. There's this feeling of "All right. Dust yourself off. Don't feel sorry for yourself. Let's keep moving." That energy and perseverance symbolizes Haiti to me. Everywhere I went on that trip, the artisans were working—and talking and joking around with each other—their hands moving nonstop as they created objects of real worth from materials of limited face value. I didn't meet one cranky artisan in Haiti. I wanted to sell enough products in the United States to be part of the effort to help these hardworking people dust themselves off and keep moving.

WILL BUYERS AT MACY'S BITE?

At the Macy's trunk show in November, six months after that buying trip to Haiti, the store finally closed at ten p.m. I stayed for a couple more hours, packing up unsold items and displays. Many employees were around, and everyone was exhausted from the holiday hours. I was exhausted, too, but also full of adrenaline. Doing a pop-up feels

INVESTING IN ARTISANS

There are a lot of ways you can make a difference in the lives of artisans, even beyond your own purchasing power. Here are a few ideas.

Get in on the Ground: Want to work at or create an artisan cooperative in Haiti or another part of the world? You can start by volunteering with a reputable group in a location that interests you. Write to the cooperative leader about your interests and skills. The group might need photography, marketing, packaging, manufacturing processes, computer programming, teaching (English, computer skills, financial literacy), mental and physical health care, or childcare. Artisan groups offering social services almost always need help, even if it's just for the short term. Some offer a stipend. Volunteering will help you decide if and where to commit full-time and how to start a cooperative yourself. It also helps you more effectively represent the work of the artisans to American buyers.

Host a House Party: Traveling to a country with a rich handicraft tradition? Leave room in your suitcase for artisan creations. Back home, rather than regale your friends with tales of your travels, invite them over for a house party and sale. Serve drinks and hors d'oeuvres and sell the fifty bracelets (or earrings or scarves) you bought abroad.

Take It Online: Go one step further and set up an inexpensive online store through Shopify or Etsy. Snap photos of your finds, include the story of their origin, and *voilà*! Instant store! While traveling, tell the cooperative that this is a one-time purchase so the artisans know what to expect. If you decide to continue, communicate your buying strategy (one purchase for the whole year or more frequent installments) to enable the artisans to plan.

like putting on a play. I'd been the director and producer, and now I was sweeping the stage and picking up dropped M&M's. I was also wheeling the unsold goods downstairs on a dolly to load back into my car. I felt like we'd done what we'd come to do. We'd generated buzz. We'd engaged shoppers. We'd even run out of some things, like the cow horn bowls and spoons from Atelier Calla and the gold leaf bracelets I'd designed in Croix-des-Bouquets.

I drove back to Harlem, where I collapsed on the couch in front of the TV with my friend LeAnne and watched a holiday movie. I was physically tired, but also elated. We'd shown that there was a serious demand for our goods, and it was Christmas in New York.

A week or so later, I got a call from Macy's. Our sale was a success. They wanted to place an order for spring, a selection of items from various artisan cooperatives we'd shown, including the gold leaf bracelets, spoons and papier-mâché ornaments from Haiti, bags and beads from Uganda, and more. It was an order for thousands of dollars' worth of jewelry and home goods. They would be priced, tagged, and displayed at Herald Square that spring.

I was so excited that I actually spun myself around in my office chair. Then I immediately called Nathalie Tancrede in Haiti to share the news. She picked up the phone, and when I told her, we both just started giggling. It was such a feeling of wonder to land this order—like we'd pulled off something huge and beaten the odds.

And it mattered: The order would help provide a few months' worth of employment for about a hundred people in Haiti. Because one person's livelihood affects many others, those employed artisans would further support about five hundred more. The order could do so many different things for various artisans. It could pay for drinking water for one artisan family for a month, and employ the guy who drives the water truck. It could be used to buy food from a local vendor, and pay the school entrance and exam fees for the artisans' children. (A hundred dollars covers school and exam fees for two children for a year.) It could also pay the guy who buffs the kids' school shoes and the taxi driver who takes them to school. (There aren't school buses, and many of the artisans don't have cars.) The order could pay for much-needed medical supplies for some, or help cover the cost of a generator for a small business. Businesses and artisan co-ops need portable generators in places where there isn't electricity, or even where there is because the island's spotty electric grid can cause constant production delays.

The Macy's order is part of what I believe to be a changing tide in Haiti—or can be, if we focus on sustainability and increasing product lines. There's been growth in the artisan sector since the earthquake, largely due to the work of the ABN and other collaborations between international designers and Haitian artists. But the same folks who bought in 2011 need to keep buying today. We can help by sharing information about the artistry and spirit of our close neighbors and by buying their goods.

As I hung up with Tancrede, I thought about who I wanted to tell next. I now had a place to send my friends from business school who often asked where they could see To the Market products in person—Macy's. The collection would be in the store by March. I picked up the phone once again, with Mother's Day presents in mind. I was excited to share the news of a new way to give gifts that give back.

SOCIAL IMPACT GIFTS FOR EVERY OCCASION

Even if you don't have a designated gift budget, you probably spend more money on presents than you realize. More than a quarter of Americans spend eighty dollars or more on a birthday present for their significant other. Most of us also buy presents for parents, children, siblings, friends, and co-workers. Here are a few ways to choose gifts that give back.

- **Baby Gifts:** Sari Bari, which employs female human trafficking survivors, has some of the cutest block-print baby blankets I've seen—as a gift, they celebrate new life for the baby and for the woman who made the blanket. You can order online at To the Market. Or check out Baby Teresa, an Australian company named after Mother Teresa that sells classic-looking fair trade onesies, bibs, hats, and blankets made from 100 percent organic cotton, and donates one-quarter of profits to groups that empower women from pregnancy to parenthood.
- **Father's Day:** Two of my favorite go-to gifts for guys are socks and ties. The sock company Conscious Step creates stylish, organic cotton socks that support different causes, matching appropriate styles to specific donations. I particularly like the men's tidal-wave-pattern socks that include a donation to the nonprofit Oceana, which protects oceans. I got my father a set of six socks, with proceeds going to causes he cares about, including ending hunger and planting trees. Tie company Reddendi sells handcrafted silk ties (and pocket squares and cuff links) with lovely, understated designs. Reddendi has partnered with the Africa Educational Trust, and one tie pays for one year of school for a child in South Sudan, Somalia, Uganda, or Kenya. Reddendi has similar educational partnerships in Syria, India,

and Peru. Neck & Tie Company's fashion-forward casual and wedding ties (that could go head-to-head with Hermès) support one specific person or family at a time. (Check online to read individual stories.)

- **Mother's Day:** In case you can't get to Macy's Herald Square to check out To the Market goods, log on to Every Mother Counts, a nonprofit started by one of my heroes, Christy Turlington Burns. Every Mother Counts is committed to making childbirth safe for mothers around the world. The charity partners with popular brands to put together a new collection of great gifts each Mother's Day that help support the cause.
- **Wedding Presents:** Heartful.ly—a company started by my friend Kate—allows couples to create a registry filled with charitable projects, like sending a girl to school in India or supporting foster children in the United States. Now you can also create a birthday registry on this site.
- **Birthdays, Valentine's Day, and Everything Else**: If you know what he or she or you like but don't know how that present helps the planet, check out DoneGood.co, a start-up that makes it easier than ever to put your dollars to work for a better world. Install the DoneGood Google Chrome browser extension on your desktop, browse Amazon, Google, or any big-name retailer for your object of desire, and DoneGood will show a socially responsible, planet-friendly alternative.

CHAPTER THREE

YOUR LATTE CAN IMPROVE LIVES

How Coffee Fuels Economic Development

Humanity runs on coffee.

—UNKNOWN

Eerie acoustic music—the soundtrack from a popular snowboarding movie—plays overhead at Cuvee, a coffee shop located in a former post office in Austin, Texas. A few people sit around the industrial-looking space, working on laptops or chatting; others are at the metal counter outside in the sun. They're all drinking one of the coffee shop's two daily offerings, custom brewed by an earnest, tattooed barista while you wait. She grinds and weighs the beans in a small countertop machine made by Baratza, then deposits them into a pre-moistened paper cone fitted into a glass Chemex carafe. Hot water flows over the beans from a black contraption that looks like an arched banker's lamp fitted with a special showerhead-like sprayer designed to uniformly wet the beans.

Two cards on the counter offer intel about the beans: "The care with which the mother/son team produce their coffee," one of the cards states, "is unlike anything we have seen. The mother, Bedhatu Jibicho, is eighty-five and has been growing coffee her entire life. We hope you enjoy the fruits of her labor." There are also tasting notes for this brew from Ethiopia: "Banana, peaches, and honey."

You can also grab a cup of the pre-brewed Spicewood blend, a mix of Central American beans. Cuvee has its own roaster in the Texas Hill Country and retails beans sourced directly from farmers in Ethiopia, El Salvador, Guatemala, and Colombia. The company also wholesales to the grocery chain H-E-B, Whole Foods, and other coffee shops around town.

Austin has a reputation as a foodie town, but you can go to coffee shops like this across the country and meet baristas and owners who similarly pride themselves on knowing the origins of the beans—in cities from Boston to San Diego and Atlanta to Zanesville. Your local roaster might have a personal relationship with specific farmers, or only offer beans that are certified organic or fair trade. You can also order coffee online that has been vetted by half a dozen popular certifications, each of which guarantees that these beans have been grown according to specific labor, environmental, and/or social requirements.

I love coffee—the taste of it, the routine of it, the variations. I love how going out for coffee is a bonding experience. I love how it's part of so many people's days, at pretty much every income level. My devotion to coffee started back in high school. The all-nighters I pulled were partly fueled by whatever cheap, canned coffee I could find. I'd often get up before dawn to bike to Tom's coffee shop near the school, joining the factory workers who also started their day at Tom's. I'd install myself in a booth with a toasted blueberry muffin and an endless cup of coffee, poured by Tom himself, who always made me feel supported while I studied. (I'd sometimes get up and pour coffee for other customers as a study break if he got busy.)

In college at Georgetown University, my love for coffee increased along with the workload. During the end of my junior year, I started working at the U.S. Department of State during the day, taking night classes to complete my degree. I'd followed after my father both in going to Georgetown and in working for the government while in school. I admired him so much and wanted to model his industriousness; I definitely relied on daily (and nightly) coffee infusions to keep up the pace.

As an adult, when I travel through places like Nepal and India to visit workshops and aftercare facilities, I always bring along packets of micro-ground instant Starbucks. I never want to get stuck facing an energy meltdown without coffee. Tea and soda don't do it for me, and it's not hard to find hot water and a cup!

After I started To the Market, I gained a whole new appreciation for coffee because of its robust supply-chain transparency. Coffee has one of the most transparent supply chains of any commodity in the world—and certainly more transparency than is available when shopping for apparel and accessories. This transparency is a model for what I want to see happen in the artisan industry and in the retail supply chain as a whole.

The artisan industry, the second-largest economy in the developing world, simply doesn't have the meaningful, consistent connection between the producers and the consumers that exists in the agriculture sector (the most significant commercial activity in the developing world). In the artisan space—and the retail apparel, accessories, and home goods industries—there's been less investment in programs to improve the lives of workers and to protect the environment, and less demand, to date, from consumers for ethical sourcing. I find this frustrating, but I continue to look toward coffee as a guidepost for where the fashion industry can go.

Coffee is something many of us rely on and spend money on *daily,* without fail. Exact consumption numbers are hard to pin down, but globally, we consume something like six hundred billion cups of coffee a year, and that number is growing as people in China and India become more devoted to the wonder of our daily brew. It's produced by people living in some of the poorest regions of the world, in a band on both sides of the equator, basically between the Tropic of Cancer and the Tropic of Capricorn. More than 25 million smallholder farmers grow coffee throughout Latin America, in Africa and Asia, and 125 million people rely on the coffee industry for their livelihoods.

Coffee helps so many of us remain optimistic in the face of real troubles, or in the pursuit of our own dreams. In one study published in the *Archives of Internal Medicine*, women who drank four or more cups of coffee a day were 20 percent less likely to be depressed than study participants who weren't downing so much joe (a stat that makes perfect sense to us serious coffee drinkers).

I sometimes buy coffee multiple times a day. And I'm not alone in this level of commitment. In the United States, we spend $40 billion on coffee each year. Is coffee at least partly responsible for the remarkable energy and ingenuity of American business? I'd say, "Yes!" Because of its popularity and supply-chain transparency, coffee is the easiest way for so many of us to use our purchasing power for good.

THE POWER OF POPULARITY, AKA "THE STARBUCKS EFFECT"

When I'm traveling, I am always excited and often relieved to spot a Starbucks nearby. I'm a longtime fan of Starbucks, but in recent years, I've definitely met coffee lovers who will avoid the corner Star-

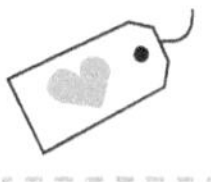

THE COFFEE-ADDICT-IN-TRAINING STARTER KIT

Just in case you need more encouragement to sit down and have some coffee, here are the basic tools to get you started.

Coffee Scoop: Digging out coffee grounds—or deciding how many scoops should go into each pot—may be more of an art than a science, which is why having a coffee scoop that is a piece of art isn't a bad thing. Some of my favorites are those long enough to reach the bottom of the bag, like the wooden scoops made in Guatemala (and sold online at places like Farmer to Farmer or One World Projects). Some people insist on a copper scoop for flavor purity; U.S.-based coffee roaster Stumptown Coffee Roasters sells a great version crafted in Japan.

Brewing: French press or automatic drip? Pour-over or stovetop espresso maker or Nespresso mini or Keurig? The debate rages in the coffee-drinking community. Different forms of preparation have pros and cons, including how long it takes to brew (French press loses); the taste, consistency, and control (pour-over wins); how long you need it to stay hot (drip with warmer pad wins); and ease of use (Keurig or Nespresso wins). I like Grosche's Dresden eco-friendly French press, made with 50 percent recycled plastic material and packaged with 50 percent recycled paper. Enthusiasts also swear by the simple design of the Chemex glass pour-overs.

The Right Mug: It's hard to beat drinking from a good old-fashioned ceramic mug. Papillon in Port-au-Prince makes nice-to-hold mugs of Haitian clay, many adorned with encouraging words, such as *hope* and *strength*. For a cup on the go, I like Homeboy Industries' insulated metal tumblers with lids, printed with phrases like *Jobs not jail* and *Kindness is the only strength there is.* A non-branded, microwave-friendly option is Aladdin's Transform travel mug, made of recycled plastic and available at Target.

bucks because it's owned by a large corporation. They'll even cross the street to go to a local shop instead. I support the desire to invest in local entrepreneurs, of course, but as it relates to coffee, Starbucks has been a supply-chain game-changer.

Almost everyone in the coffee industry—from growers in Guatemala to coffee sellers and experts in the United States—credits Starbucks with popularizing the idea of spending nearly two dollars on a cup of coffee and paying attention to where the beans were sourced. I delight in this fact because I enjoy drinking Starbucks and because, as anyone who has stood in line for a tall vanilla latte can see, Starbucks proves it's possible to source ethically and remain a business success for decades. These wonderful, quirky, independent coffee shops around the country—charging far more than the fifty cents I paid at Tom's coffee shop in high school—are thriving, in part, because Starbucks has created a demand for high-quality coffee. A whole supporting industry of coffee accessories and brewing paraphernalia has also sprung up as a result of the market for high-quality, ethically sourced brew.

Starbucks always had an interest in ethical sourcing. In the 1990s, it joined forces with Conservation International (CI) on a project in Mexico that has wound up improving the coffee crop, and farmers' lives, around the world.

Conservation International is a thirty-year-old nonprofit whose mission is to protect the planet for those who live on it, both humans and other animals. In the late 1990s, CI was working to protect a critical area of biodiversity in Chiapas, Mexico, on the southern tip of the country, bordering Guatemala. The region had been designated by UNESCO's Man and Biosphere Programme as a critical area of biodiversity. CI was looking to encourage low-impact agriculture in a protective buffer zone around the reserve because without economic opportunities for people who live near protected lands, environmental initiatives can falter. As Bambi Semroc of Conservation International explains, resentment can build if you protect land or animals *instead* of people rather than *with* people. "I saw this when I was a Peace Corps volunteer in northern Togo," she says. "People were forced off their land to create a protected area, which created animosity. When democracy happened there, the people went into the park and killed the animals in retaliation."

Coffee is a great crop from an environmental perspective, because it can grow in the shade of other, taller trees. Coffee trees can be planted underneath the existing canopy—basically by thinning the forest rather than clear-cutting it. Other types of farming rely on clear-cutting massive swaths of forest to plant crops, which damages the environment in a number of ways. Coffee farming seemed like a perfect buffer zone activity in Chiapas because the region already had a tradition of shade-grown coffee under old-growth, native trees.

CI launched a project to increase coffee production in Chiapas, then sought opportunities for the farmers to sell their beans to roasters who valued good environmental and social practices. CI reached out to various roasters and coffee companies. Starbucks was immediately interested in the story, and had a big market. But when the "cuppers" tasted the coffee from the beans, they found the quality lacking. Instead of abandoning the idea, Starbucks worked with CI to improve the coffee grown by these farmers and, along with it, the farmers' income.

The Starbucks team taught farmers in Chiapas better harvesting and processing techniques, such as picking only the red, fully ripe cherries. Coffee actually comes from a fruit—a round, pulpy berry about the size of a grape, called a cherry. Fully ripe cherries are usually bright red or a deep burgundy (though some can be yellow or orange). Beans inside ripe cherries have a far better flavor than those picked when the cherries are unripe or only partially ripe. The cherries themselves have a surprisingly delicious, sweet flavor, a little like watermelon crossed with rose or maybe passion fruit. You never see coffee cherries because the real kick (and value) is in the beans—two hidden inside each cherry.

Starbucks also helped the farmers choose the best postharvest technique, which really impacts the final flavor. There are a few different ways to handle the postharvest of coffee beans, but the main distinction is between dry and wet processing. With the dry method of processing, freshly picked cherries are spread out on a huge surface under the sun and turned throughout the day for several weeks, until the moisture content drops to 11 percent (and the cherries are shriveled like raisins). The beans are then removed from the dried fruit.

With the wet method of processing, the beans are removed from coffee cherries right after picking by a huge pulping machine. The beans, still covered in a slick mucus, float down a series of water channels and through rotating drums—like a Disney Splash Mountain ride for coffee beans. Then they are fermented for twelve to forty-eight hours, rinsed, and dried under the sun, on drying tables, on mesh platforms, or in large tumblers.

The Chiapas program was a huge success. Starbucks began buying from Chiapas and then working with CI to replicate the project around other critical conservation reserves. They began projects in Peru, Costa Rica, Panama, Colombia, and Indonesia, adapting the best practices to each country. Eventually, the Starbucks team realized it needed a standardized set of growing, harvesting, and drying practices, leading to the creation of Starbucks's own coffee-verification program, called C.A.F.E. Practices, in 2004. C.A.F.E. stands for "Coffee and Farmer Equity" and is a system of growing guidelines based on

101 CERTIFICATIONS
WHAT'S BEHIND THE LABEL

There are a handful of certifications today signifying that the coffee (or chocolate or snack food) you're buying was made sustainably—but their exact meaning can be unclear to consumers. The fact that these labels exist has real value; while they all signify slightly different things, each one guarantees that the seller or manufacturer is trying to source in a way that protects farmers' livelihoods and the environment.

Most certifications require a third-party auditor to inspect the farm and processing facility. This can be a thorough investigation that ties up everyone involved for a week and requires showing records of things like seed sources, soil conditions, and weed and pest management approaches. Certifications are also a way for coffee bean brokers to differentiate between lower-quality beans and something special. These certifications enable farmers who follow the requirements to ask for a higher price for a superior product. (One important exception is "all natural," a marketing phrase that isn't tied to any actual certification program.)

Below is an explanation of the most common certifications you might see on a bag of coffee.

Bird Friendly: Coffee from Latin America that is grown on farms providing a good habitat for birds, as in, not clear-cut land.

C.A.F.E. Practices: Starbucks has invested more than $100 million in improving the social and environmental impact of coffee growing. This includes its own verification system called Coffee and Farmer Equity (C.A.F.E.). C.A.F.E. is not a seal you can see on the bag but a behind-the-scenes way for Starbucks to establish and monitor good growing techniques and pay farmers more for them. This includes providing farmers access to capital, support services, and even carbon-reduction programs. Some other companies also will pay more for the high-quality, C.A.F.E.-verified beans.

Direct Trade: This means coffee was sourced by the roaster from the farmer, without middlemen. The theory behind direct trade is that the buyer and seller have formed a mutually respectful relationship, agreed on a fair price, and avoided losing profits to a third party or obscuring the origin, as happens with commodities. It's a growing movement in the coffee industry, as evidenced by the little handwritten cards describing the farmers' lives at Cuvee and the full-color photos of farmers on the walls in so many Starbucks locations. With a single-element product like coffee beans, a company such as Starbucks or the 110-year-old New York–based roaster/wholesaler/retailer Porto Rico Importing Company can buy directly from the farm or farming community.

It's much harder to do direct trade, at this point, with artisan goods. An artisan group in Kampala, Uganda, for example, could theoretically produce products directly for Macy's, but they need help with quality control, tagging, and meeting Macy's workplace standards. These needs are part of why there are so many middlemen in fashion, and why a group like To the Market is needed to bridge the gap.

Fair Trade: Many consumers have heard of this certification, which is primarily focused on empowering small-scale farmers and producers who lack the bargaining power of large corporations. These small farmers can be vulnerable to accepting whatever price they can get for their product, from whoever happens to come along. Rob Everts, co-executive director of Equal Exchange, the oldest and largest 100 percent fair trade coffee roaster in the United States, explains it like this: "Our purpose on this planet is to reform trade. We want to inject equity wherever possible, and to level the playing field between desperate rural farmers and buyers in the U.S. and Europe." Equal Exchange, which started in 1986, does about $70 million in sales today. You can buy Equal Exchange coffee, chocolate, and other products online and in stores across the country.

You'll find fair trade labels on everything from coffee and chocolate to clothing and home goods.

The Germany-based Fair Trade Labelling Organizations International (FLO) was established in 1997. The U.S. branch of FLO is called Fairtrade America, but you'll also see "Fair Trade USA," a splinter group based in Oakland, California. All fair trade standards are designed to tackle poverty and empower producers in the world's poorest countries. To get either label, producers must have democratic decision making and a say in how the fair trade premiums are invested. There must also be social programs in the community, decent wages, freedom to form unions, no forced or child labor, and adherence to health and safety standards. The fair trade environmental aspect looks at factors such as minimal and safe use of agrochemicals, soil fertility, and water resources, and no use of GMOs. Farmers can get an additional premium for organic growing.

Fair trade has a long history, and it's fascinating to read about. It's getting some pushback today from people who think the acceptance of large tea plantations into Fair Trade USA has watered down its mission. Some craft chocolate makers say the fair trade certification has limited value because it doesn't indicate anything about the quality of the cacao beans. Still, both the Fair Trade USA and Fairtrade America labels mean that a third-party, independent auditor has verified that the coffee (or other product) was grown or produced according to a set of standards governing the trade relationship between the farmers and traders.

Rainforest Alliance: This international nonprofit network of farmers, foresters, scientists, governments, environmentalists, and businesses is dedicated to conserving biodiversity and ensuring sustainable livelihoods for the people working the land. To get the label with the little green frog, a farm must comply with ten standards of the Sustainable Agriculture Network (SAN), including ecosystem conservation, wildlife protection, and fair treatment and good working conditions for workers. If you see the seal, you can rest assured that this coffee (or other product) was grown and harvested using environmentally and socially responsible practices.

USDA Organic: If you buy a bag of Peet's Coffee, you'll see a round logo printed on the front that says "USDA Organic." Small print on the back reads, "Certified Organic by QAI." What does this mean? A lot, it turns out. The United States Department of Agriculture Organic stamp is the federally established protocol for growing and/or processing crops, meat, and packaged foods. To be USDA Organic, a farm can't use synthetic pesticides or fertilizers or GMOs and must be inspected every year by a third-party auditor authorized by the federal government, such as QAI—Quality Assurance International, a San Diego–based company established in 1989 that is one of the largest certifiers in the world. A USDA Organic farm must follow organic guidelines for three years before getting the round label; for coffee farmers, this means transitioning to all-organic growing (if they're not already doing so) and being able to provide proof of this history for three years.

With meat, organic regulations require animals to be raised in decent conditions that respect their natural behaviors, such as grazing land in the case with cows. Animals must be fed 100 percent organic food and be raised without antibiotics or hormones. Processed foods can't contain artificial preservatives, colors, or flavors and must have organic ingredients (though there are some approved nonagricultural ingredients in certain foods, such as enzymes in yogurt, pectin in fruit jams, and baking soda in baked goods). A packaged product that says, "Made with organic ingredients" must have at least 70 percent USDA Organic certified content.

UTZ Certified: This certification program, launched in Guatemala in 2002 by a Belgian Guatemalan coffee grower and a Dutch coffee roaster, aims to increase the amount of coffee being certified globally from both small and large farms. UTZ certification also applies to cacao, tea, and hazelnuts. To become certified, suppliers have to follow a code of conduct focusing on good farming methods, working conditions, and environmental sustainability. Although many people have never heard of UTZ, it's currently the largest certification program for coffee and cocoa in the world. UTZ merged with Rainforest Alliance in 2018 with the goal of establishing and using a shared certification process in 2019.

principles similar to other certification programs, such as fair trade and Rainforest Alliance. More than a million farmers and coffee workers have participated. By 2015, Starbucks verified that 99 percent of its coffee was ethically sourced.

MAKING COFFEE THE WORLD'S FIRST SUSTAINABLE CROP

Some coffee growers and lovers are worried about the future of our favorite bean because of environmental and market volatilities. Conservation International estimates that hotter summers and changing rain patterns could slash the world's current coffee-growing area in half. Quality coffee is grown in the mountains, and even if farmers respond to rising temperatures by planting higher, the amount of available land decreases as you get toward a mountain's ever-narrowing peak. Already, warmer temperatures in the mountains have led to the spread of a fungus called coffee rust. This fungus, which has been attacking the leaves of coffee trees since the late nineteenth century, recently appeared in high-altitude areas that had long been safe due to their relative cold, devastating coffee crops in Mexico, Guatemala, and El Salvador.

Meanwhile, most coffee beans are traded as a commodity, making farmers vulnerable to market fluctuations. The price of beans depends on supply rather than demand because the demand for coffee basically never drops (an obvious truth to coffee drinkers like me). A new supplier in the market can slash the commodity price for farmers everywhere, as happened in the early 2000s, when the market was flooded with inexpensive beans. Producers in Guatemala, for example, suddenly faced a market in which the cost of growing beans exceeded the price they could command. This devastated the local economy and drove many people out of the industry in search of better-paying work.

Conservation International and Starbucks have banded together once again to fight these threats to our morning cup of joe. In 2015, they launched the Sustainable Coffee Challenge during the Paris climate meetings. The Sustainable Coffee Challenge, which has grown into a huge collaborative effort by private companies, governments, nonprofits, and research institutions, aims to make coffee the first sustainable agricultural product—and to ensure that we'll have enough coffee to fuel our futures. The program has three arms. One is to improve the livelihoods and economic prosperity of coffee farmers, their families, and coffee-industry workers. The second focus is on increasing productivity to meet future demand. The final goal is to prevent the clear-cutting of even one additional hectare of valuable forest or the depleting of other natural resources for the growing of coffee. So far, more than one hundred partners in more than two dozen countries have committed to the Sustainable Coffee Challenge, including McDonald's, Walmart, and the Specialty Coffee Association.

In 2016, Starbucks also launched an initiative called One Tree for Every Bag. For every bag of coffee sold in its stores, the company donated the cost of a new coffee tree (about seventy cents) to Conservation International, which then worked with partners on the ground to plant trees in Guatemala, El Salvador, and Mexico. Coffee trees start to decline in productivity when they're about twenty years old, and farmers need to refurbish their fields regularly to guarantee a good yield and decent earnings.

Starbucks, Root Capital, the Fairtrade Access Fund, the International Finance Corporation, and the Inter-American Development Bank have together committed $50 million by 2020 to something called the Global Farmer Fund. This fund will provide affordable access to credit for coffee farmers and cooperatives, a key component of being able to invest in things like new trees, make changes to meet certification requirements, and market the beans.

COFFEE FARMING IS FOR GIRLS

Because of the decades-long efforts at supply-chain transparency in coffee, you can actually go to a major coffee-growing country like Guatemala and see how your dollar does good. Guatemala, a Central American nation of sixteen million, bordered by Mexico to the north and the Pacific Ocean to the west, produces some of the world's best coffee, and has long been a supplier for Starbucks. The land here looks like a bunched-up blanket—hills going every which way and

DRINK UP!

A good cup of coffee is freshly brewed from flavorful beans and enjoyed at a favorite spot, perhaps with a favorite person. But a *great* cup of coffee also helps make the world a better place. You can harness your caffeine craving for good by drinking at one of these spots.

- **A 2nd Cup (Houston, Texas):** Located where I was born and raised, this coffee shop uses a portion of its profits from coffee to fight human trafficking in Houston, a major hub for international and intranational trafficking in the United States.
- **bwè kafe (Hoboken, New Jersey):** Started by Maryanne Fike and her family, largely in response to the 2010 Haiti earthquake, bwè kafe serves La Colombe coffee and actively supports college education for Haitians through Love for Haiti, access to clean water through Coffee for Water, and Haitian farmer training in partnership with La Colombe.
- **Blue Bottle Coffee (Oakland, California):** Indie favorite Blue Bottle sold a majority stake to Nestlé in 2017 for an estimated $500 million, a sign that the market for coffee with a rich story behind it is in high demand. You can find Blue Bottle in its original state of California or in newer locations across the United States and Japan, including New York, DC, Miami, and Boston.
- **Camano Island Coffee (Camano Island, Washington):** This social-impact coffee company is known for organic beans, shade-grown plants, and fair wages. You can also buy a blend that gives a portion of proceeds back to a nonprofit. My favorite is the Set Free blend, which supports the anti–human trafficking organization Set Free, a To the Market partner.
- **City Bean Roasters (Los Angeles, California):** This 100 percent family-owned, Los Angeles–based coffee shop distributes 20 per-

cent of its after-tax profits to its staff, regardless of position. It also donates all coffee chaff (a waste product of the roasting process) to local farmers and gardeners.

- **Counter Culture Coffee (Durham, North Carolina):** This roaster buys from cooperatives around the world, sells online, and now has training centers that offer Friday morning tastings in thirteen cities. A 2012 Green Plus Sustainable Enterprise of the Year Award winner, Counter Culture runs a sustainability program called SEEDS (Sustaining Environmental and Educational Development at Source) that donates to coffee-producing partners and their communities. The company sells great coffee, including Sipacapa from Guatemala. Counter Culture is also a founding member of the Coalition for Coffee Communities—an organization addressing food security issues in coffee-growing communities.

- **Fire Department Coffee (Rockford, Illinois):** Founded by a pair of U.S. Navy and Marine veterans-turned-firefighters, this Illinois-based coffee roaster sells reasonably priced, roast-to-order coffee online and donates a portion of proceeds to a different firefighter- or military-related charity every other month. Cofounder Luke Schneider says the company grew out of his love for coffee, and his dislike of so much of what was offered at the fire stations. "At the station, there is a lot of what I consider really bad coffee. Mass produced. Sitting on the shelf a long time. Firefighters rely on coffee to keep them going. We wanted to create something that was fresh, enjoyable, and good enough to drink all day long." Their Original blend is a mix of Central and South American beans.

- **Starbucks Reserve Roastery and Tasting Room (Seattle, Washington):** This upscale version of your corner Starbucks showcases rare coffees. There are locations in Seattle and Shanghai, and stores are slated to open in NYC, Tokyo, Chicago, and Milan. You can also find mini Reserve bars in many existing Starbucks.

- **Thrive Farmers Coffee (Atlanta, Georgia):** This for-profit is transforming the coffee supply chain through an innovative revenue-sharing model that eliminates the toxic volatility of the commodity market. Thrive also minimizes the number of brokers in the chain and maximizes the income to the farmer.

steep valleys cutting off towns, making travel difficult. You see an occasional volcano rising up in a perfect triangle, its tip pointing through the clouds.

Guatemala is known for great coffee and poor roads. Even the main throughway in the relatively developed southern coast has sections pockmarked with potholes. Smallholder coffee farmers who grow the most prized "strictly hard bean" coffee (brewed from beans grown at least 4,500 feet above sea level) often live in small communities high in the hills, accessed by dirt roads which can be completely washed out in the yearly rains. Many are members of the twenty-two indigenous tribes descended from the Mayans, who retain their traditional ways.

The lack of transportation infrastructure is one reason that many Guatemalans struggle to find economic opportunity and to send their children to school: both can be too hard to reach. Guatemala has some of the highest poverty and lowest education rates in the Western hemisphere, at least among the indigenous farmers living in the remote highlands. There's a great deal of inequality in Guatemala, and traditionally, most of the vulnerable people live in the rural communities in the hills. Many of these farmers have only one or two acres and are subsisting by growing just enough for their own families, and often not even that.

...

For Maribel Tojil Sanchez, a mother of two living in Sipacapa, a super-remote community in the western highlands, learning to grow high-quality, certified organic coffee was a game-changer in her life and that of other women in her village. It takes Sanchez about seven hours to get down from the hills of Sipacapa to Quetzaltenango, the country's second-largest city—a charming, historic, high-altitude place that feels a little like Quebec City with its cobblestone streets, historic stone buildings, and great coffee shops.

On a bright November weekend, just before harvest season in the northern hills, Sanchez traveled to Quetzaltenango to talk about how coffee farming has benefited her village. She was wearing a traditional woven dress adorned with blue flowers and a scalloped neckline decorated with beads, and a Western-style navy blazer buttoned over the top. Her long black hair was curled and pulled back in a ponytail. She had the focused, somewhat fatigued air of someone who is busy and who just took a long journey early in the morning to share her story and her gratitude for the opportunity she's had.

The impetus to farm coffee in Sipacapa came from an unusual place. For decades, residents looking for work had to travel long distances to other parts of Guatemala, or even Mexico—a common reality for indigenous people in the hills. The need to travel for jobs kept members of this community and others like it constantly moving, isolating families far from the support of their relatives and pulling kids out of school year after year to accompany their parents. More recently, people from Sipacapa and other parts of the country have headed to the United States in search of the far higher wages available for manual labor here. (As of 2017, money sent to Guatemala from relatives working in the United States reached nearly $7.5 billion.)

In 2008, a mining company came to Sipacapa and proposed to buy up all the locals' land to build a coal mine in it and then hire them to work it. Despite their constant hustle to find work, the townspeople didn't want to sell to a mine. A neighboring community had done that, and seen a rise in alcoholism and violence. As Sanchez explains it, rejecting the mine felt like fighting for their cultural integrity. "Our culture is not like that. We did not want that. Our culture is different," she says.

Still, turning down the opportunity of the mine forced the community to take a hard look at their ongoing economic struggles. They needed a way to make more money. Subsistence farming of corn and cows not only made them vulnerable to outside pressures but also kept the community locked in instability, poverty, and illiteracy. Sanchez only had a middle school education because her family lacked the resources to send her to high school. Although the first six years of basic education are theoretically free and mandatory in Guatemala, secondary schools are scarce outside the cities, especially in rural indigenous areas. People often have to travel far distances to continue the basic education that we in the United States take for granted, and many can't afford the trip. The expenses for middle and high school can make it prohibitive even to those who live near one.

Sanchez, a single mother with a five- and ten-year-old at home, was working all the time to make ends meet when the mining offer arrived. She knew that if she kept going as she was, she couldn't guarantee that her son and daughter would have any more education or opportunity than she'd had. Many of the people in her village had similar stories.

But what else could they do? They reached out to the local Catholic church for help. The church assisted the community in resisting the mine company's offer and worked with local leaders to analyze the potential of their land. The conclusion? They could grow high-altitude, strictly hard bean coffee in those hills. The market for high-quality, hand-picked coffee was growing in Europe, Asia, and the United States. The higher price that these beans command could mean far better profits than those available through traditional crops, letting them earn money without having to travel for work.

With the help of a Dutch nonprofit called Solidaridad, the community got training in coffee farming and founded a local association to allow all participating new coffee growers to have a say in their organization and decision making. They decided to raise Bourbon and Caturra, two varieties of the high-quality Arabica beans.

Right away, the local women assumed important roles. Coffee farming starts with making large seed beds in a nursery and tending to the seedlings for a full year—watering them and protecting them from direct sunlight. The community decided that caring for babies—even baby plants—was women's work. This decision transformed the lives of the women. Working in a plant nursery turned out to be a great vocation for mothers, Sanchez says. It's less physically demanding than other forms of agriculture, and babies and toddlers can hang out with their moms in the nursery all day. After school, older children can help with the work, watering the plants and learning how to tend them.

When the time came to sell the fledgling coffee trees to locals eager to try coffee farming, the women suddenly found themselves holding real assets. They had raised the plants and they were the ones who earned the profits from the sales, after reimbursing their local coffee association for the seeds. The women earned more money than they ever had before. They suddenly had more economic power, and valuable skills, and soon became leaders in the cooperative—and in the community.

With the help of the same Dutch nonprofit, the Sipacapa community planted its first crop of trees at the end of 2009. It takes about three years for coffee trees to bear fruit, and Solidaridad provided critical economic support during this pre-harvest period. The coffee farmers picked their first crop of coffee cherries at the end of 2011. They joined a larger cooperative called Manos Campesinas, based in Quetzaltenango, that exports beans for organizations of small farming communities. In 2013, through Manos Campesinas, the Sipacapa community exported 11,700 pounds of single-origin, super-high-quality beans labeled "Sipacapa." By 2016, they had improved the quality of the beans and had more plants in production, enough to ship 160,900 pounds of coffee through Manos Campesinas.

Sanchez says it was hard to get some men to listen to the women in the beginning, not only because of their gender but also because they weren't proven coffee farmers. But once the community saw the results of their labor, farmers became eager for the women's input. Sanchez was elected vice president of the cooperative's board in 2012 and has held leadership roles ever since.

All Sipacapa coffee is grown according to organic certification requirements, a practice that Sanchez says is better for everyone. "You can see the difference now that we're doing all organic farming. With more chemicals, you stopped seeing the other kinds of plants. Vegetables didn't grow. Now I can grow tomatoes and lots of other vegetables."

You can order Sipacapa online through Counter Culture, which buys from Manos Campesinas. If you do, your morning brew directly supports Sanchez, her children, and an entire community that has tapped into the power of decent-paying work to lift itself out of poverty and to help give women more of a voice. Today, nearly a third of the cooperative's 238 members are women, many holding leadership roles. Sanchez works as a coffee "promoter," encouraging farmers to plant coffee, showing them how to care for the plants, and instructing them on better growing techniques.

As Sanchez says, "Before, parents would give their money or land to the men. Now it has changed; money and land can go to the girls, too. Now we see women in the local government, as authorities in their community. It's changed for many reasons, and coffee growing is one of them."

I love this story because it shows how private business, along with nonprofits, absolutely can transform lives for this generation and the next, and change long-standing gender dynamics.

SUPPORTING SMALLHOLDER FARMERS

Manos Campesinas is a success story itself. Manos Campesinas works with about 1,400 smallholder, indigenous farmers in the highlands of southwestern Guatemala, including areas around Guatemala's Lake Atitlán. Nearly a quarter of its members are women, including the current board chairperson. The cooperative was founded in 1997, the year after the peace accords were signed, finally ending this nation's thirty-six-year civil war. The idea of smallholder farmers banding together for more bargaining power had been gaining traction, but during the civil war, these efforts were complicated by the larger Cold War. Indigenous cooperatives could be mistaken for guerrillas and killed.

After the civil war ended, Manos Campesinas got to work in earnest. The cooperative received funding and training from Hivos In-

HOW TO SPEAK GOOD COFFEE

Coffee is an industry with its own language, much like wine. Luckily, picking up a few key words can be enough to get by.

Cupping: This is a term you hear a lot if you start hanging out with coffee producers. Coffee is repeatedly tested for quality and taste. This process is referred to as "cupping" and usually takes place in a room specifically designed to facilitate the process.

Species: The two main commercially grown species of coffee are Arabica, which is generally higher quality, and Robusta. Arabica comes from the highlands of Ethiopia, eastern South Sudan, and northern Kenya. Robusta, from low-lying regions in Africa, is grown largely throughout Brazil and is most commonly found in less expensive, canned coffee.

Strictly Hard Bean: This term generally refers to coffee grown 4,500 feet above sea level or higher. Higher-altitude beans take longer to mature, which translates into denser beans with more robust flavor and a higher price.

Varietal: You'll hear people use the word *varietal* to mean "variety" or "cultivar," but coffee bean purists insist that *varietal* should be used to describe coffee beans after they have been brewed. A lot of people know the term *varietal* from wine; a varietal is made from a specific variety of grape, such as merlot, which gives it a specific taste and profile.

Variety or Cultivar: A natural or hybridized subspecies of a coffee plant. Coffee's flavor is affected by the land where it's grown, the harvest and postharvest techniques used, and the exact variety of the plant. There is a growing awareness of different flavor aspects of different types of coffee plants. The original varieties of Arabica are Typica and Bourbon. Caturra, which grows throughout Guatemala and has been shown to be susceptible to the fungus coffee rust in the country's lower regions, is a natural mutation of Bourbon, which was first found in Brazil. Both coffee and cacao researchers hunt for new and ancient varieties the way prospectors look for gold—the goal is to increase the varieties available to improve flavor, disease resistance, and sustainability.

ternational and Oxfam, two international independent aid agencies, to help it meet some specific goals. These included having all the affiliated farmers meet the requirements for organic certification, introducing yield-increasing techniques, improving the quality of the coffee so it could compete in the international market, negotiating the best price, and using profits to support member organizations' specific social and economic objectives.

In 1998, farmers affiliated with Manos Campesinas shipped their first container of coffee beans outside of Guatemala—about forty thousand pounds of fair trade, certified organic coffee—to the Netherlands. In 2000, Manos Campesinas began a relationship with the U.S. roaster Equal Exchange, which greatly expanded the cooperative's market and enabled it to export thousands of pounds of beans to the United States each year. Today, you can buy Equal Exchange coffee sourced from Manos Campesinas online, as well as in some Target stores, and in about three hundred food co-ops and family-owned small food chains.

Within a decade of its founding, Manos Campesinas had become a fully self-sustaining business, no longer receiving any support from nonprofits. The sales director is a hardworking, driven, forty-something Guatemalan named Miguel Mateo. Mateo grew up in an indigenous community in northwestern Guatemala, and learned Spanish as a second language and English as a third. He is dedicated to finding markets that will pay smallholder, indigenous farmers at least twice the commodity rate for their coffee beans. He sees the growing market demand for high-end, hand-picked beans as absolutely critical to improving the livelihoods of smallholder farmers. "Our best partners are small- and medium-sized coffee roasting companies that are focused on quality and have the objective of helping alleviate poverty. These are the most reliable in terms of paying a fair price to farmers even if the market or weather fluctuates," he says.

How does Mateo convince potential buyers to pay double the commodity rate for super-high-quality beans? He brings them to the farms to see just how much work goes into getting coffee from the tree to the cup.

To visit the farm of Miguel Ajsoc Chacom, for example, a smallholder coffee farmer living near the shores of Lake Atitlán, you have to drive for several hours from Quetzaltenango, then head down a concrete road full of switchbacks in the deep jungle to the charming little town of Santa Clara La Laguna. Like most of the towns around Lake Atitlán, Santa Clara La Laguna is populated almost entirely by people of Mayan descent. The women wear elaborate traditional dress—in this case, beautiful, long, woven pencil skirts with multicolored vertical stripes; wide belts embroidered with flowers; and solid-colored, short-sleeve blouses with square necklines decorated with embroidery and beads. The town is calm and quiet in the steady afternoon sun. While Lake Atitlán is a popular tourist destination, this entire region has maintained its rural character and traditional ways.

You park on the edge of town, then hike uphill for about twenty minutes on a narrow dirt path under the hot sun through low jungle. Dried stalks of corn rise impossibly high toward the piercing-blue sky.

Ajsoc Chacom takes this hike every day to tend to his farm. During harvest season, he carries bags of coffee cherries down the hill on his back, or sometimes on a horse.

Ajsoc Chacom is thin and fit, with a deeply weathered face and a big smile. He's wearing navy chino pants; a long-sleeve, collared shirt; and a navy baseball cap with the Nike logo. He speaks with pride about his farm, giving specific details about each plant, the way you might share your enthusiasm about your own backyard garden with neighbors. He points out the year-old coffee trees, the local avocado species, the temporary shade trees he planted while waiting for the wide-canopied shade tree called Chalum to mature.

"It's one hundred percent, one hundred percent organic," he says with a wide smile as he explains how each plant contributes throughout the year—providing shade, making mulch, serving as holiday decorations. He leans against a skinny temporary shade tree, pointing to a six-foot-tall poinsettia tree in full bloom. "My farm tells me Christmas is close. The farm is like an education every day."

Later, in his small, concrete-floored house, while sipping coffee that is sweet enough to drink black if you normally take sugar, he explains that he never had any formal education, never went to school, "not even for an hour and a half." He grew up in Santa Clara La Laguna speaking Quiche, his dialect. As a child, he traveled with his family to the coastal plantations where his parents would pick cotton, sugar, and coffee, which prevented him from attending school.

He didn't learn to speak Spanish until he was twenty-four. Word had gotten around that he was hardworking and smart, and a nonprofit leader reached out to him to help run a plant nursery that the group was starting in the region. When Ajsoc Chacom complained that he couldn't possibly remember all the names of the plants because he didn't speak Spanish, the nonprofit employee challenged him, saying,

"I do not accept that excuse. If I accept that excuse, I am pushing you over the edge of a cliff." Ajsoc Chacom decided to learn Spanish, picking up the language simply by listening, because he hadn't been taught how to read and write. (His wife, who makes herbal remedies for babies in town, still primarily speaks Quiche.) That challenge changed his life, as did the money from the nursery job that speaking Spanish enabled him to keep, and the help of two grown sons who moved to the United States and send remittances back home.

You meet so many people like this in Guatemala, hard workers with obvious natural intelligence and drive but incredibly limited opportunities for education and for work. It's inspiring to hear stories like that of Miguel Ajsoc Chacom, but also sobering to think of how easily he could have gone through his whole life without these opportunities.

Later, Miguel Mateo talks about another difficulty facing coffee farming—young people giving it up in favor of easier urban occupations or a shot at working in the United States. Manos Campesinas is now focusing on motivating young people to stay with farming by highlighting the real economic opportunities available in agriculture by taking an organic, fair trade or direct trade route and working with buyers who believe in economic development throughout the value chain.

Miguel Mateo also shared his own efforts to get an education. He dropped out of school after ninth grade because his town lacked a secondary school, and his mother couldn't afford to move to the larger town of Huehuetenango, to the north, where the closest school was. His father had been killed in the civil war, and his mother had to take care of the family on her own. He was able to return to school the following year and eventually, with stops and starts, to finish high school. Six years later, he went to college with help from an educational NGO that partnered with the university, then got the job with Manos Campesinas.

It's heartbreaking and eye-opening to hear how hard the young (and not-so-young) people in this beautiful, misty, peaceful-feeling nation struggle to get themselves to school. The civil war left about 200,000 people dead, everywhere along the economic spectrum. In many cases, the loss of a parent complicated the already-challenging process of getting to school or supporting a family.

With so many of the success stories, relatively little was required to change the course of someone's life—whether it was an NGO that helped with school or a nonprofit that offered community training and funding to tend new crops until harvest. The impact of small interventions like these points to how our purchases can have a huge ripple effect in a country like Guatemala. What seems like an insurmountable barrier for so many could be removed with an amount of money that, for many of us, is pretty small.

SPENDING THE BUCKS FROM STARBUCKS

While smallholder farming is an important sector in Guatemalan coffee farming, the country also has plenty of medium- and large-sized coffee farms, or fincas, often owned by members of the same family for a century or more. These larger farms provide steady and seasonal work for thousands of farmers across the country, and their owners also point to the certification process as a key to keeping them afloat by allowing them to differentiate between their high-quality, hand-picked beans and those harvested mechanically in other countries.

For Finca Los Andes, a nearly two-hundred-year-old coffee planta-

GIVE A HAND-UP IN GUATEMALA

Guatemala is a land filled with incredible potential and people who have strong ambitions to create better lives for themselves and others. It takes such a small amount, in U.S. dollars, to turn around someone's life. Here's how you can help:

Cover the Cost of Going to School: Help someone start or finish school with nonprofits Mayan Families or the Global Education Fund.

Order Guatemalan Coffee: Order the coffee for your office or home from a cooperative in Guatemala that follows certified organic, Rainforest Alliance, or fair trade practices, or that has a direct trade relationship with a roaster you trust. Check out Manos Campesinas, Kishé's Woman-Grown blend, and De la Gente Guatemala.

Support Farmers: Donate to VisionFund International's microfinance or Heifer Project International's sustainable farming initiatives to help women farmers around the globe, including in Latin America.

Support Farmers' Children: Donate to Funcafé, the social services fund that is part of Anacafé, Guatemala's national coffee association. Funcafé focuses on health, education, food, and nutrition for Guatemala's rural population. A donation can also pay for a water filter, which dramatically reduces disease, and environmentally efficient, safe woodstoves. You can also propose a specific program.

Sponsor a Scholarship or School: The relative scarcity of high schools makes it hard for many Guatemalan youth to continue past sixth grade and makes it more likely that they will start work rather than focus on studying. Funcafé has a "coffee high school diploma," which includes a high school education and classes on coffee growing. A scholarship could go toward this program or another. You or your company can pay to build a school for those in a rural area through Funcafé.

tion blanketing the southern slope of the Atitlán Volcano, selling to Starbucks has brought stability, higher earnings for farmers, and essential income during the coffee market crash of 2001. In the midst of the crash, Starbucks signed a three-year contract with the finca, agreeing to a guaranteed premium price, enough above the commodity price to enable the farm to keep running. (This contract also helped Starbucks's business, since it ensured their own supply of beans.) Starbucks again helped in 2011, when coffee rust attacked huge swaths of the finca's trees. Finca Los Andes pays workers more than they'd earn elsewhere as temporary labor, in part due to the premium it gets from Starbucks for following the company's C.A.F.E. Practices verification program.

Finca Los Andes has more than one thousand acres, one-third of which are cultivated for coffee, tea, macadamia nuts, and other produce, and two-thirds of which are held as a nature preserve. Although Los Andes is located in the relatively developed southern coastal region, the farm itself is remote, at the end of a very long, unpaved road deep within the rain forest. It takes four hours to get there from Guatemala City, over a twisting, often rutted road. Steep walls of rosy earth rise up on either side, blanketed with dense, low-lying jungle, spilling over with tangled vines. The countryside is intensely green, with very little development outside the main cities, although you do see small communities that have sprung up along the main road, catering to travelers heading from Guatemala City to Lake Atitlán or to the colonial town and tourist favorite Antigua, or on to Mexico.

About an hour west of Guatemala City, there's a pineapple farm and a dozen pineapple stands lining the road. Drivers pull over for an afternoon snack. They stand in the dirt on the side of the road, biting into dripping chunks of pineapple, the juice trickling down their chins. Everyone in this rural land seems to be working all the time,

COFFEE AND CULTURE IN GUATEMALA

Most visitors to Guatemala head to Antigua, an inland valley town five thousand feet high, ringed by volcanoes, and filled with Spanish colonial architecture from the seventeenth and eighteenth centuries. The Antigua you see today was built in 1543 on a grid pattern inspired by the Italian Renaissance. It served as the capital of Guatemala until 1773, when an earthquake destroyed much of the town, inspiring the nation's leaders to move the capital to Guatemala City. This move left Antigua's amazing architecture undisturbed for centuries, while the development and modern building trends happened in Guatemala City. Antigua remained essentially frozen in time, which means that today, you can turn a corner and see an incredibly ornate Spanish-style cathedral rising before you, half in ruins, perhaps with a small, bustling coffee shop built right into the structure.

When I arrived in Antigua for the first time, I was blown away by how beautiful the town is, with its cobblestone streets lined by low, painted, stucco buildings, and the way it sits in this valley in the shadow of volcanoes. Every few blocks, you see a massive white stone monastery, school, or a beautiful old church with an elaborate hand-carved facade. The artisan peddlers, dressed in their traditional Mayan woven garb, set up a daily craft market located inside a crumbling seventeenth-century church on the town square.

After doing a little shopping (and stopping for coffee), you can see how coffee is grown just outside Antigua at the Filadelfia Coffee Plantation tour. You can also stay on Filadelfia's property, which feels more like a Spanish colonial estate than a farm. In town, check out El Convento, a boutique hotel across from the Convent of Capuchinas, a historic convent from the 1700s.

You can also learn about the history of chocolate, a crop grown there for centuries, at one of several ChocoMuseos in town. Hot chocolate was an important ceremonial drink in Mayan culture, and you can taste a version of this ancient drink made with chile and cinnamon.

Quetzaltenango is a less touristy city high in the hills with crisp mountain air, amazingly preserved architecture, and coffee shops on every corner. Quetzaltenango is known for Spanish-language schools, and there's a student vibe there, with books on international development left on shelves in coffee shops, and late-night restaurants and bars.

Another popular tourist option is to visit the charming Mayan towns surrounding Lake Atitlán. Most of the people in these small towns have retained their Mayan clothing, customs, and language.

doing anything they can to generate extra income. You see people carrying wood on their backs, running little roadside *tiendas*, working in the fields. They're up early and on the job. In other countries in Latin America and the Caribbean, running late is almost expected and can seem like a point of pride. But in Guatemala, nearly everyone arrives early; a driver scheduled to pick you up for a meeting at eight a.m. may well show up at your hotel at seven thirty. There's a feeling of constant industry and effort.

In *I, Rigoberta Menchú*, the classic memoir/group narrative of the indigenous Guatemalan experience under generations of repressive regimes, the author describes the incredible work ethic of the Mayans. Menchú (who won the Nobel Peace Prize in 1992 for her efforts to promote equal rights for indigenous people in Guatemala) speaks with pride about the fact that at age eight, she could pick coffee beans without breaking a twig and haul pounds of coffee herself. Still, despite this culture of work, there are not enough good jobs to go around.

When you finally get to Finca Los Andes, by cutting through a rubber plantation at the end of a rocky road partway up the volcano, you see low coffee bushes with ripe red cherries growing under the shade of the taller Chalum trees. The coffee cherries at this altitude turn red earlier in the season than they do higher up. A string of simple houses are clustered together about a mile into the property. The finca employs nearly fifty full-timers, all of whom live in these airy, tin-roofed houses with concrete floors, woodstoves, and running water. For full-time employees, housing comes with the job. Because it is so hard to get to, Finca Los Andes is one of the few remaining coffee plantations that still houses pickers right on the farm. It also has a school, health clinic, two churches, and a small store for the farmers and their families. Another twenty-five part-timers come during the harvest to help pick.

The property also has a main house that now serves as an office and occasional lodge for visitors. It's a long, gracious, ranch-style home built by the previous owners, with wood-beamed ceilings and windows facing a terraced hillside. There's a huge wooden table in the dining room, and couches and books—as well as a framed copy of the finca's first contract with Starbucks hanging on one wall. From the back patio of the house, you can gaze out at the mist rising off the Pacific Ocean and feel both the history and the changes happening here. You can hear someone stacking bricks elsewhere on the property, the crow of a rooster, and the rushing of the stream that powers a water turbine generating electricity for the whole estate.

Owner Jim Hazard and his late wife, Olga, bought the farm in 1985. Today, in his mid-eighties, Hazard is soft-spoken and gentle. He's a Guatemalan of British descent. Hazard still participates in some activities but leaves most of the work to his son-in-law, Jaime

Freire. They both live in the old estate house a few days a week, basically camping out in the property; technology allows much of the business to be run from the city.

Los Andes currently sells much of its crop to Starbucks, and both Hazard and Freire thank Starbucks for keeping coffee standards high. "There are not so many Starbucks," Freire says, speaking about such a large company being so focused on quality and farmers' livelihoods. "We still sign three-year contracts with them."

The school for the farmers' children is near the main house, and a newly planted section of coffee trees, courtesy of Starbucks's One Tree for Every Bag program, stretches out just past that. Finca Los Andes received twenty thousand new trees of a varietal that has been shown to be more resistant to coffee rust, and earlier that year, planted three thousand of the new baby Starbucks trees in this gently sloped twelve-acre plot. Each new tree went in next to the stump of an old Caturra tree that had just been cut down.

By November, the Starbucks trees were two feet tall, squat, bushy coffee plants with super-shiny oval leaves. It's amazing to have heard about this promotion at the local Starbucks in the United States and then to see these trees, now a little more than a year old, planted in neat rows under the shade of tamarind trees and skinny, white-barked Palo Blanco trees that resemble Dr. Seuss's Truffula trees.

Work begins early on the finca for both the farmers and their families. On a Friday morning in November, about thirty children sit in the two-room schoolhouse, grouped in "learning teams" of five students each around old, wooden teachers' desks painted pale pink and mint green. Colorful poster-board projects hang on the walls, and books line a shelf in the corner. The building itself is like a large garage—concrete block walls, tin roof, and open windows without screens. But the atmosphere is warm and supportive. The huge front door remains open all day, offering a view of the lush, green hills. The kids can hear chickens in the distance, someone sawing wood, the bark of a dog. They may even catch a glimpse of their parents walking by. A hand-hewed picket fence painted in bright primary colors, like crayon sentinels protecting the learners, surrounds the school property.

The school also has a chicken coop and vegetable garden. This garden contributes to education and health. Vegetables are not traditionally a big part of the Guatemalan diet, and the idea here (also popular in the United States) is that growing green things can help get kids excited about eating them. The kids cultivate the onion, pepper, cabbage, and bean plants and collect the eggs from the little amber-colored chickens every day. They sell half the eggs to the on-site market to pay for chicken feed, and eat the rest during the school day.

The school is partly funded by the finca and partly supported by Funcafé, the nonprofit arm of the country's national coffee association, Anacafé. Funcafé provides books, teacher training, and guidance on what should be included in a recommended, nutritional ten a.m. meal.

The typical indigenous diet of corn and beans lacks a variety of nutrients—and these days is often "supplemented" by packaged junk food. Seven out of ten children of Mayan descent still suffer from malnutrition—even if they're not hungry—because of this deficit. Malnutrition contributes to stunted growth, lowered immunity, cognitive delays, behavioral problems, and learning difficulties, all of which can impair school performance and limit future job opportunities. Funcafé helps families learn to prepare and eat more balanced meals.

The kids at this farm school look healthy; they've already had their ten a.m. brunch and seem eager to start learning. They're dressed in clean, matching white-collared golf shirts with the school's logo and jeans or skirts. In addition to their balanced daily meal, they are also visited at school by a full-time paramedic who serves as the community doctor. He teaches the children basic hygiene, delivers babies in the community, tracks the health of the workers, ensures that everyone has taken the annual pill that protects against river blindness, and runs an on-site clinic.

A second, smaller room at the school is reserved for the first graders. Sitting at one of the low tables are two sisters from the highlands, Bima and Rosalia. Bima, aged eight, has a round face with a smattering of tiny freckles and big, wide-set eyes. She's quick to smile and sits leaning forward, watching the teacher. Rosalia, age ten, has long, shiny, black hair braided in a thick rope that she wears to the side. Both sisters jump up when asked to perform a song they've learned, excited to share something they know.

Most of the kids their age are in the larger main room, but these sisters sit with the first graders because they had no schooling until their father got a job at the finca. Their parents, Pablo Gutierrez and Felipe Alvarez, come from a small, rural community about seven hours away in Quiche, a mountainous region that is considered the heart of the K'iche' people. Neither Gutierrez nor Alveraz ever attended school.

As an adult, Gutierrez found work as an itinerant picker of coffee and cotton, and the entire family would leave the village every year for his jobs. At one point, he landed steady work at a big farm, but there was no school nearby, and the one in the next town was too far. The bus cost about $40 US per month, which was three-quarters of his take-home pay after expenses. So the girls didn't go to school.

Gutierrez tried to get to the United States twice in search of better-paying work. He was so desperate for work that he sold his own small farm in the highlands, using the money to pay a smuggler or "coyote" to help him cross to the United States. He was caught by border guards in Mexico and sent back both times. After his second failed attempt, he had nothing left. He found work at Finca Los Andes as an itinerant picker.

Gutierrez is an industrious, consistent worker. Freire got word of his strengths and hired him as a full-time employee. This meant a house, and all the services the finca provides. Moving to the farm—which requires workers to send their kids to the free on-site school—provided his daughters their first-ever chance to learn.

This is exactly the kind of social change that can happen through ethical purchasing, and it's so exciting to see. If you buy a cup of Guatemalan coffee from Starbucks, you are directly helping to support the teachers sitting with the kids at this school and others like it. The finca gets an even higher price from small, independent coffee roasters who buy its highest-quality, higher-altitude strictly hard bean coffee. A cup of Guatemalan coffee from Coffee Emporium in Cincinnati (or through their online store), from Coffee By Design in Portland, Maine, or from your room in some Radisson hotels also contributes to the lives of this nation's families and future.

Funcafé's budget comes from grants and annual fees that Anacafé collects from all affiliated coffee producers in Guatemala. This means that you are helping these kids and others like them basically any time you buy Guatemalan coffee from anywhere. This is especially true when you pay a good price to a roaster who is ethically motivated or to a coffee shop offering certified or direct trade Guatemalan coffee.

Coffee is the largest provider of jobs in Guatemala's rural areas, and some finca owners like Freire see a thriving coffee industry as the best way to encourage Guatemalans to stay in the rural areas and in their own country. "It's better to stay here, in my opinion," says Freire. "You have a simple house, a school nearby. Better than moving to the city where you have one room and maybe a job far away and a school in a dangerous area."

On Saturday, the Los Andes school is open, and several teachers are administering an exam to the older kids. One of the exam administrators, a short, confident-looking young man named Nelson Ruiz, grew up on the farm and attended the school himself. His sister is one of the main teachers during the week. Ruiz finished one year of college. "I'd like to do more, but it costs a lot of money," he says, a common refrain among people young and old in Guatemala.

That day, Bima and Rosalia are at home with their parents and their two younger brothers. The house is quite modest by American standards, but Bima and Rosalia's mom says she's grateful to have wood, electricity, and running water to be able to wash the clothes. A lack of steady housing with basic amenities like clean water can make it hard to take care of a family and contributes to diseases that sap nutrients, another factor in malnutrition.

Alvarez holds her hand in front of her mouth as she smiles, covering her missing teeth. She and her husband have been here nine months and still seem to carry the weight of their struggles with them. Gutierrez says he hopes to stay put until all the kids are eighteen and have finished school. "I want the girls to make up for the lost time," he says.

Reliable employment with a conscientious company, and the school and health services that come with it, are the turning point out of generational poverty for this family. Bima and Rosalia, who are staring out the window as their parents talk, and their two little

CALIFORNIA COFFEE: THE NEXT NEW VARIETAL?

While coffee plants have historically thrived only in countries straddling the equator, one coffee entrepreneur in California is trying to change that. If you dream of buying a 100 percent made-in-America cup of joe, coffee-preneur Jay Ruskey, the first commercial coffee grower in California, has the answer.

Ruskey owns a forty-two-acre farm high in the hills above Goleta, an agricultural region two hours north of Los Angeles. For the past fifteen years, Ruskey has been refining coffee farming in California. In recent years, he's begun training other local farmers in organic, hand-picked coffee growing. His company, Frinj Coffee, sells farmers the trees, consults with them on growing and picking, and buys the beans to ferment and roast himself. He envisions a California coffee-growing region as robust and award-winning as the state's wine industry. Sound impossible? So did the idea of vineyards blanketing the hills of California years ago.

"You're not supposed to grow coffee in California. You can't do it," says Ruskey, pointing to the stout coffee plants with their thick, shiny leaves and bright red cherries covering his hillsides. "I'm a disruptive technology."

His farm is perched high above the Pacific, past deep green, rolling hills. Coffee plants grow in rows in the distance, red-earth pathways winding in between. The farm also grows avocados, dragon fruit, passion fruit, and caviar limes. It looks like Shangri-La, an idyllic, fantasy kind of place. Shaggy-frond Washingtonian palm trees rise up beyond a small lake near the tasting room, where Ruskey and his wife, Kristen, welcome visitors for occasional scheduled tours and tastings.

At one such tasting, held during harvest season, a half-dozen coffee tourists sit on stools at a raw wood counter, listening as Kristen explains the coffee-making process. They also touch plants, sip coffee, view equipment, and taste the coffee cherries fresh from the tree. A few branches lie on the counter. One type has cherries so red they're almost burgundy, while another variety has orange cherries that look like shiny kumquats. Coffee cherries have a jelly-like consistency and delicious flavor. Each cherry has two pale green coffee beans inside. The farm's roaster, a shiny metal barrel with a huge funnel on top, sits quietly in a corner.

The air up here is cool and amazingly clear—an ideal climate, Ruskey insists, for coffee. It's far cooler than nearer to the equator and has some very rare frosts and a fog that blankets the hillsides on summer mornings. Much like wine grown in the northern regions, California coffee has a unique flavor profile, due to the longer time it takes for the cherries to ripen in this cooler clime. Cherries sit on the trees for about a year up here, which can be twice the growing time near the equator. The harvest season here is between May and September, varying slightly each year due to climate patterns. Then the beans dry for one to two weeks and are stored until they are roasted, ideally within two to eight months of harvest.

The higher labor and land costs mean California coffee does not come cheap—at least not yet. Efficiencies in the postharvest process should help bring the price down, though Ruskey's aim is to produce the highest-quality coffee feasible, not low-priced, commodity-traded coffee. "In my perfect world, we're doing it in the best way possible, and this will help reduce the price," says Ruskey.

As is the high-altitude, hand-picked, organic coffee in Guatemala, California coffee is part of the specialty coffee market. What this means is that you'll pay more but will be supporting sustainable agricultural and economic practices that benefit farmers and help forge the development of a new U.S.-based agricultural product. Creating new growing regions is another way to sustain the industry into the future. Ruskey hopes to create a California coffee brand and maintain tight quality control to ensure that consumers will ask for it by name, the way a wine lover might ask for a chardonnay from Napa Valley or a pinot noir from Sonoma County.

Ruskey insists that every high-end cup of coffee helps create more awareness of what goes into coffee generally. "I think it brings light to the fact that this is a process that takes the work of many people. It's raising awareness of how much labor goes into coffee, that there are farmers in this chain, and that their lives and livelihoods matter. We take a farmers-first approach. We're focused on our farmers and making sure they get a good wage and are rewarded for doing good-quality coffee."

brothers, who are by now bouncing on the bed, are like kids anywhere. Stable work for their parents gives them a chance to grow up with the comfort that comes from not having to worry about where they'll sleep, when they'll eat, or how to get an education.

I see the growing demand for high-quality, sustainably sourced coffee as a percolator of food security and educational opportunities for families like those in Guatemala and around the world. It also helps bring the self-esteem that comes from dignified work. A core part of To the Market's business model is the belief that economic opportunity creates independence and personal agency, and this connection is easy to see with coffee.

Coffee is also central to my own personal daily functioning. Most mornings, I speak to our director, Danielle, and our COO, Jill, during our nine-thirty call. It's three hours earlier in California, where Jill lives. We'll be setting out the day's priorities, and Jill will often say, "Okay, I'll get to that after I've had some coffee." Danielle and I are usually two cups in by then. Knowing that our coffee habit helps send girls like Bima and Rosalia to school adds an extra kick to my morning brew.

HOW TO BREW A PERFECT CUP OF COFFEE

At Good Land Organics coffee farm in Goleta, California, trained cuppers use a pour-over system for tastings because it allows for the hottest water and most control over how the water flows through the grounds. Here's how to be your own cupper.

- Grind your beans immediately before brewing.
- Moisten the paper filter by pouring hot water over the entire thing and letting it drip through. Discard the water.
- Pour hot water in the carafe to preheat it. Discard the water.
- Place the coffee grounds (2.5 tablespoons for just under two cups of water) in the filter.
- Heat water to 105 degrees Fahrenheit, then pour a small amount on the grounds to allow them to bloom.
- Pour the remaining water slowly and consistently over the grounds to allow them to continue to swell as the coffee drips through into the carafe.
- Serve!

CHAPTER FOUR

WHY REINVENT THE WHEEL WHEN YOU CAN REPURPOSE IT?

Finding Real Value in Overlooked Places

There is no such thing as "away."
When we throw anything away it must go somewhere.

—ANNIE LEONARD, SUSTAINABILITY ADVOCATE

I was having dinner with my husband, Nate, standing at our kitchen island, eating pizza out of the box. The TV news was on in the background and Nate was holding a slice, telling me about an exciting new partnership his company had with the grocery store chain Wegmans.

Nate is a natural storyteller and delights in sharing tidbits he thinks I'll find amusing. He'll say, "Did you see that such-and-such happened?!" Or, "Guess what I read!" He has a great memory for details and retains huge amounts of trivia. I have a notoriously bad memory for minor facts, and it's nice to have a spouse to turn to when I need to know who said a famous quote or what song played in a specific episode of the nineties TV show *Beverly Hills, 90210*.

Nate is from Kentucky, and shortly after we married, we moved into an apartment in downtown Lexington as our home base. We were both traveling so much and so focused on building our businesses that we weren't sure where we wanted to settle. We decided to just rent a one-bedroom and choose a permanent place later. We found an apartment in a three-story redbrick building—a converted factory with retail stores on the ground floor, and an amazing coffee shop called A Cup of Common Wealth. Our apartment had seriously high ceilings, granite countertops, and never quite enough light.

On that night in Lexington, Nate was telling me about a recycler his company had found that could take discarded Wegmans uniforms—the collared golf shirts and khaki pants that most grocery store employees wear—and turn them into beds for dogs and cats.

Nate founded and runs a technology company in the waste and recycling space called Rubicon Global. It focuses on using business solutions to solve the growing problem of trash. Rubicon links companies seeking trash removal to independent and local garbage haulers who work with composting operations, anaerobic digesters (which produce energy from waste), and creative recyclers like the one making pet beds. He named the company after the Rubicon river that Julius Caesar famously crossed. Even back then, in ancient Rome, Julius Caesar had to confront removal and recycling of food and human waste, and disposal of statues (by melting them down). Caesar turned to civil engineers for help creating a sewage system. Naturally, Nate found these historical facts fascinating.

Companies today are increasingly setting zero waste goals—basically eliminating trash sent to landfills or incinerators. Rubicon helps them meet these goals, while also making trash disposal more efficient and cost-effective. Rubicon also aims to reduce the number of trash trucks on the road by collecting only when a client really needs it. This is a very different philosophy and approach than that taken by the largest industry players in the United States, which tend to just dump everything into landfills, which they often own. Rubicon

GREAT RECYCLED, SUSTAINABLE PRODUCTS

Many large and small companies are working to create products that protect the environment by reusing materials. Check these out:

Bloomerent.com: This company "recycles" flower centerpieces from weddings, corporate events, and other big affairs. You work with a florist affiliated with Bloomerent to create your centerpieces; after your event, the company resells your used flowers to someone nearby, and you get 10 percent back. Or, contact Bloomerent to see if there's an event near you that will have centerpieces to recycle when you need them; a Bloomerent florist will customize the flowers for you and deliver them—saving you 40 to 60 percent off the retail price.

Decomposition Notebook: Need a new journal, a notebook for school, or just a place to make lists? Instead of your usual college-ruled notebook, check out Michael Roger's "decomposition books," cool notebooks with eighty pages of 100 percent post-consumer-waste paper, printed with college-ruled lines in soy ink. Each book has a different design—the ocean, the cosmos, or the rain forest. Available online, at Whole Foods, and at Target.

Green Toys: This California-based toy company makes colorful plastic fire engines, airplanes, tea sets, and toys from 100 percent recycled materials, including gallon milk jugs. All toys are made in the USA and surpass U.S. and international standards for no BPAs.

Grove Collaborative: Our friends at Grove have created an eco-friendly subscription service for the best household products on the market, like Seventh Generation, Method, and Mrs. Meyer's cleaning products. The company focuses on recycled packaging and carbon offsets for shipping.

Old Saw Ventures: This network of barn dismantlers sells wood from abandoned barns to designers, builders, and individuals who are remodeling homes or commercial spaces. Many people love the look of reclaimed lumber and the increased strength and stability that come from the aging process. The wood often can be sawed into wider planks than newly harvested lumber. It's a fabulous way to add character to a home without cutting down trees.

Patagonia: The company's recycled polyester collection ranges from puffy jackets to backpacks. Aesthetically, you would never know that each piece contains fibers made from recycled soda bottles, manufacturing waste, or worn-out garments.

Reformation: This Los Angeles–based fashion-forward company manufactures sleek, chic, upscale women's clothes in California with environmentally friendly Tencel and viscose, fabric scraps, and upcycled vintage clothing. There are stores in NYC, California, and Dallas so far. Online orders come with free shipping.

Scenery Bags: What happens to those elaborate sets created for Broadway shows? If you buy a Scenery Bag, they could wind up hanging from your arm. Jen Kahn, a stage manager for years, created Scenery Bags as a way to prevent beautiful backdrops from being dumped into the trash at a show's end. Kahn collects discarded backdrops from set rental companies and theaters—including those that have housed popular musicals like *Hairspray* and *Oklahoma!*—and has them cut up and sewn into clutches. Bonus: Your bag comes with a label about the show it's from. It's an ideal gift for theater lovers (and a portion of proceeds goes to the Stage Doors program, which brings schoolkids to Broadway shows in New York City).

Teeki: This eco-conscious active wear line makes cute, super-long-lasting yoga pants, tank tops, and shorts from recycled plastic water bottles. The company is committed to ensuring that suppliers follow the California Transparency in Supply Chains Act. Available at yoga stores in California and Pennsylvania, and online.

also points to one of myriad reasons Nate and I like each other so much; we're both deeply interested in tackling social challenges through market-driven solutions.

Rubicon finds revenue streams that can be generated through recycling, such as pet beds, and shares earnings with its clients. I love animals, and I could envision comfy pet beds made from old cotton clothing. I also admired the ingenuity of this solution. These kinds of repurposing projects are such a clear display of humankind's creative potential. I'm a big believer in repurposing in general; I'll store clothes for six months to send to my cousins, who I know will use them rather than throw them away. I see recycling as a way of democratizing raw materials and gaining more value from creativity. But I've gained a great deal more appreciation for the importance of recycling since meeting Nate—not only for the sake of the environment but also for lower-income communities here and abroad.

THE GLUT OF GARBAGE

I know that trash hauling may not sound fascinating, but the status quo of waste disposal is creating a growing environmental and social crisis. The U.S. waste industry has historically been dominated by three enormous companies that own trash trucks and landfills. They make an overwhelming majority of their profits in "tipping fees," what they charge for dumping, or "tipping," garbage into their landfills. They're more like real estate companies in this regard, incentivized to maximize profits by routing all possible waste to their landfills.

Landfills are massive in-ground or aboveground containers that are some of the worst polluters in the country. There are different kinds of landfills for different materials, and they are regulated by the Environmental Protection Agency (EPA). Still, as a whole, landfills are the third-largest producer of human-related methane emissions in the United States. Methane gas traps heat in the atmosphere even more than carbon dioxide does. Decomposing garbage also leaks toxins into the air, contributing to higher mortality rates in areas where landfills are built. We create at least 3.5 million tons of solid waste a day, globally, which is ten times more than we did a hundred years ago. Here in the United States, we each toss roughly the equivalent of our own body weight every month. Most of this ends up in landfills. Since most people don't want to think too hard about their garbage, it's been easy for these three major companies to dominate the space and refuse to innovate for decades.

The five hundred or so landfills in the United States are built in some of the poorest communities in our country, meaning they're potentially harming people who are already struggling. Once a landfill goes in, other companies tend to be driven out. No one wants to build a housing development, shopping mall, or even a factory near a landfill. Nate sees the trash industry as the environmental justice issue of our time. As he says, "Basically, when a landfill comes to an area, everything else around it dies." Housing prices plummeted by 50 percent after landfills were built in poor neighborhoods in Cleveland, outside Detroit, and in Milwaukee.

THE D-I-Y ZERO WASTE HOUSEHOLD

How can you create less waste at home? The EPA has established a "waste management hierarchy," a preferred order of disposing garbage, to help you clean up your act. Here's how the hierarchy works:

Best approach: Create less waste by buying less and using up all of what you have.

Second best: Reuse old containers, clothing, sheets, etc., in new ways.

Third best: Recycle what you can't reuse. (How many plastic yogurt containers can one family store? Not many, it turns out.)

Fourth best: Use waste as fuel by sending discards to a waste-to-energy converter or responsibly burning your trash for heat or fuel.

If all else fails: Toss it in the trash.

The good news is that businesses are actually free to choose their own garbage hauler in most of the country (a fact that most of us don't know). The technology also exists to recycle most of our trash. Europe, Asia, and Australia are way ahead of us in this regard. The EPA estimates that we bury billions in valuable materials every year. In 2014 alone, we tossed nearly $50 billion worth of recyclable materials globally. That doesn't mean people are accidentally throwing out heirloom jewelry, but rather, there is monetary value in so much of what we toss. Old cardboard can be sold to countries like Thailand to make boxes, for example. Used aluminum can easily be recycled into new cans. Steel commands a high price as a building material. Food waste, which accounts for half the trash in the United States, can be turned into fuel, feed, and fertilizer.

As Nate was telling me about his Wegmans venture, I started thinking about To the Market and our supply-chain goals. While I'm super proud of the work of our ethical producers and our To the Market team, this conversation really challenged me to think about how our artisan partners could do more with discards. I'd spent so much time working to convince individuals and major corporations to source ethically, but I hadn't given nearly as much thought to the raw materials our partners were using to make those products. How could we think strategically about making products from trash? Could we design deeper, stretch the boundaries of even the most mundane materials and our own vision for them?

Residents in the developing world are often plagued by excess trash and limited or nonexistent garbage removal. Turning trash into treasure would help with this problem and possibly become an important part of generating more economic opportunity. If I could help artisans expand the products they make from free or almost-free raw materials, I could help them create more with lower upfront costs, dramatically increasing their ability to scale up their businesses. Focusing more on recycling, or upcycling, as I like to think of it, at the artisan level suddenly seemed like a hugely important, under-realized opportunity.

I was just about to travel down to Haiti again, a country that to me exemplifies the art of making something out of nothing. As I'd seen on my first visit, many artisans use discarded products and seem to subsist on sheer resourcefulness and imagination. I'd been so inspired by the creativity and energy in Haiti. Now I was driven by a new question: Could we harness the skills of these artisans and our design eye to create totally new products from discards—items that could sell as luxury goods? Could we produce an entire line of accessories from discarded materials that a sophisticated shopper would choose instead of traditional, high-end gold or silver jewelry?

Long, dangling statement earrings were the most popular accessory for spring/summer 2017. None of our local partners were making them, and we hadn't produced any in our To the Market Exclusives Collection, a missed opportunity for us that spring. The earring trend seemed certain to continue into fall. I suddenly had a vision of dangly earrings fashioned from discarded cow horn that would look sophisticated enough to go head-to-head with those made by well-known designers working with precious metals and expensive stones.

As I got ready for my second trip to Haiti, I started sketching a few designs for earrings. I'd gained a fair amount of firsthand knowledge about what our customers like at that point, and about the process of taking a design from concept to pattern to sample. I believed we could create some outstanding shapes with cow horn, if it could be pressed thin enough and cut precisely enough by the artisans at the cooperative Atelier Calla, which had impressed me so much on my first trip.

I emailed drawings of two styles of dangly earrings to Atelier Calla. The studio's founder and head designer, Christelle Paul, promised to have samples ready on my arrival. I couldn't wait to see how they'd turn out.

FORGING BEAUTY FROM LIMITED MEANS

When I arrived in Haiti, I was reminded once again of why I consider it the queen of creative recycling. Artwork is everywhere, usually made from the humblest raw materials. I was walking into a hotel in Port-au-Prince, and I had to stop to snap a photo of a striking mosaic built into the sidewalk, two L shapes made from multicolored ceramic shards, bordered with metal and embedded in a square stone.

HOW BIG COMPANIES ARE FOCUSING ON ZERO WASTE

Corporations around the world are focusing on decreasing their negative impact on the environment. Below are a few examples.

Hilton: Travel and tourism is one of the world's largest industries, and Hilton has made aggressive commitments to helping advance the United Nations' 2015 Sustainable Development Goals, through its LightStay program. Since 2009, LightStay has helped reduce the chain's energy use by 17 percent, waste by nearly 30 percent, water use by nearly 17 percent, and overall carbon output by nearly 23 percent across its hotels. (Yes, it is worth reusing that towel a second night rather than dropping it on the floor and getting a new one.) Hilton also launched the industry's first soap-recycling program, and has recycled more than five million bars to date—that's more than one million pounds of soap waste *not* sent to landfills. To the Market has collaborated several times with Hilton's Travel with Purpose program and it's been great to see firsthand the company's efforts.

Microsoft: In November 2016, Microsoft became the first technology company to receive a Zero Waste Facility certification from the U.S. Green Building Council. The company now prevents 90 percent of waste from heading to landfills at its headquarters in Redmond, Washington, where more than 44,000 employees work in 125 buildings across 500 acres.

Procter & Gamble: As of 2017, more than half of the locations of this Cincinnati-based consumer packaged goods giant send zero manufacturing waste to landfills. P&G also diverts office paper and food scraps from landfills through employee-led programs. (The company says such staff-led initiatives allowed its Costa Rica plant to go entirely zero waste.) These moves are part of P&G's goal for all of its plants to send zero manufacturing waste to landfills by 2020.

Sierra Nevada: In 2013, Sierra Nevada's Chico, California–based brewery was certified as a platinum-level Zero Waste Facility by the U.S. Zero Waste Business Council. The following year, Sierra Nevada diverted nearly 100 percent of its solid brewing waste away from landfills, in part by sending 150,000 pounds of spent malted barley and 4,000 pounds of spent hops a day to local cattle and dairy farms to use as feed. The brewery is also home to the first HotRot composting system in the United States. Installed in 2010, the system has transformed more than 5,000 tons of organic waste into compost.

Subaru: Subaru of Indiana Automotive hasn't sent waste to local landfills in more than a decade, nor have two of Subaru's manufacturing plants in Japan. Subaru reuses everything from auto part packaging to staff food scraps. The Indiana plant alone saves an estimated $1 to $2 million a year through its reduction and reuse programs. Subaru has the best profit margin in the automotive industry, showing the economic sense of reducing waste. Nearly 100 percent of the components of a Subaru vehicle can be recycled or reused.

Target: Target's corporate social responsibility efforts include a pillar called *planet*, which focuses on climate, chemicals, water, sustainable operations, and sustainable products. In 2017 alone, Target diverted more than 70 percent of its retail waste away from landfills through reuse and recycling programs.

Toyota: A founding member of the U.S. Zero Waste Building Council and the winner of the EPA's WasteWise Partner of the Year Award in 2016, Toyota reduced, reused, or recycled 96 percent of its nonregulated waste at its North American facilities in 2015, saving more than nine hundred million pounds of refuse from winding up in landfills. As of 2017, twenty-seven of the company's North American facilities met the council's definition of a zero waste site, including ten of its manufacturing plants.

It was a handmade version of the kind of grand entrance logo I'd seen at upmarket hotels. For the most part, Haitian businesses don't have the resources to hire famous architects to design new buildings and fill them with high-end finishes like imported hardwood floors or marble facades. They wind up decorating with things they can make themselves. This leads to an exuberant kind of creativity. As the artist Henri Matisse put it, "Much of the beauty that arises in art comes from the struggle an artist wages with his limited medium." It almost feels like the entire island is an art installation, or an artist's playground. There are endless works-in-progress, and it feels very organic, the line between experimentation and completion never totally fixed.

One workshop I visited had a seating area of two low, handmade mosaic tables and matching red chairs; the walls were decorated with ten watercolor-on-paper images of men's faces. It was a comfortable rest area put together with found materials and artwork made on the island, and it had a level of natural cool that is hard to re-create at a distant design studio.

I think of Haiti as the queen of recycling also because there's no reliable trash service in the country. In the United States, we're so accustomed to putting our garbage outside and having it disappear, as if by magic. But in Haiti, most people just burn their garbage, a far-from-ideal solution, not only because it can generate toxic fumes but also because not everything burns—such as plastic. The very properties that make plastic so useful, such as its durability and resistance to degradation, make it nearly impossible to destroy.

Because most Haitians don't have access to clean tap water, they buy a lot of bottled water, and you see discarded plastic water bottles everywhere (a common sight in many low- and middle-income countries, actually). Empty plastic water bottles line the streets, along with soda bottles, chip bags, and plastic cups. Plastic floats in streams and peeks through the underbrush, where you see goats picking through it.

Globally, we've produced about 83 million metric tons of plastic, and less than 10 percent gets recycled. When plastic first became popular, after World War II, there wasn't that much of it around. But we've reached a tipping point for plastic—we have too much and we know too much to continue tossing as usual. Nearly 80 percent of our world's plastic production has wound up in landfills, or floating in oceans, or clogging creeks, or blowing in the wind in places like Haiti.

I saw a truly Haitian-style response to the problem of discarded plastic. A creative entrepreneur had come up with a way to encourage people to reduce their use of plastic bags by designing super-cute cloth bags screen-printed with illustrations of animals affected by excess plastic. The animals look like they're from a children's book—simple, black-and-white line drawings filled with bright blocks of color. I first saw one of these bags hanging in the corner of the little store in the Marriott, Port-au-Prince. It was printed with a sleepy-looking octopus with long eyelashes and curvy tentacles, and the Creole phrase *Sachè non mèsi!* which translates loosely into "Bag? No thank you!" (Who needs a plastic bag when you have this cool cotton reusable one?)

On another bag, five pink-and-gray round-bellied pigs floated through the air, each hanging on to a colorful plastic bag overhead like a parachute. A third had a cow with a sweet smile chomping a red plastic bag, a half-dozen others floating in her stomach.

The bags were being sold by an artisan cooperative called 2nd

Story Goods, which operates in the Haitian town of Jubilee. 2nd Story Goods is dedicated to helping artisans earn a living wage while strengthening their own community. I bought a handful of these bags to take home because I loved the designs and because they represented the inspired entrepreneurialism that I find so uplifting in Haiti.

Accompanying me on this trip to Haiti was one of my best friends, Rachel Faucett, a brilliant designer, owner of the family-friendly brand Handmade Charlotte, and an advisor to my company. Rachel wanted to design a collection for her label to be made in Haiti, with To the Market as the production coordinator. I was excited to have her join me because we always have a blast together, and it was great to have a partner on the island.

Rachel's oldest daughter, Izzy, was also with us. Izzy was a rising senior in high school and wise beyond her years. She was acting as my photo assistant/intern. Izzy is a natural explorer, and she was fully engaged—asking questions at co-ops and leaning in to get a closer look at the products. Izzy had traveled before and had recently gone on a mission trip with her church to the Dominican Republic. But she'd never been to Haiti. Seeing Haiti through her eyes reminded me, once again, of just how far this nation is from the United States in terms of economic development, and how much tension the poverty can create.

We were traveling around in a big, airy van with a driver who was an expert at navigating Port-au-Prince's winding, sporadically paved roads and a guide named James Samson from the Artisan Business Network. At one point, we sat parked in the van, shooting an iPhone video to upload to Facebook. A young man came up to the van and started making "I'm hungry" gestures, bringing his fingertips to his lips and staring into the window. I advised Izzy to ignore

PURGE THE PLASTIC (AND EXCESS PAPER) FROM YOUR ROUTINE

Help be the change toward less plastic on the planet by taking one of these steps, many of which can also save money.

Become a Bulk Buyer: It may be time-consuming to get started, but most cities have at least one grocery store or chain with bulk sections for nuts, grains, granola, candy, popcorn, etc. Go see what is available that you regularly purchase and commit to (a) switching to scooping out that product from the bulk bin and (b) keeping a plastic or glass container from a food product to fill with it. Once you get the hang of it, add another grocery item to your bulk list. Buying in bulk means less plastic containers used, and less money spent.

BYOB (Bring Your Own Bottle): Fill a reusable bottle with water rather than purchasing new ones, a step that helps save the planet and save you money, particularly at places with marked-up prices, like the airport. You can also bring your own mug to coffee shops or the office. (Some coffee shops will even give you a discount!)

Grab Your Bag: A growing number of grocery stores sell reusable shopping bags, many of which are made of eco-friendly materials. Stock up on a few of these, which usually retail for under ten dollars, to avoid accumulating a pile of plastic bags in the kitchen that eventually get thrown away. It can take one thousand years for a plastic bag to degrade. To the Market offers ethically made, affordable, reusable bags to consumers and retailers alike. If your local store doesn't offer an alternative to plastic, buy one elsewhere, and encourage this addition.

Just Say No: Refuse all kinds of things you don't actually need, such as layers of tissue paper a cashier might wrap around a new sweater you're buying before putting it in the bag or paper versions of your bills (who wants those anyway?) that can now be sent electronically. When ordering takeout, you often wind up with an entire second bag of napkins, straws, and little packets of ketchup or soy sauce. Ask for your food without these additions, and use your own utensils and condiments at home instead. If you can stand it, skip the plastic straw.

him, a suggestion I felt conflicted about making. But none of us can help everyone all the time, even in a place with so much need. We didn't have food with us in the van, and we also needed to think about our own security.

This experience really brought to the forefront the complicated issue of how best to help. All of us seeking to make a difference in the developing world have to balance our good intentions with pragmatic approaches that actually work. This is particularly true in Haiti, where there has been a long tradition of aid efforts gone awry. It seemed like half the people on our plane ride down were missionaries, which is common on flights to Port-au-Prince. They came from churches and nonprofits alike. It's awesome that so many people want to help, and it makes sense for churches specifically, since Haiti is the poorest country in our hemisphere and about 80 percent Christian. And yet, in some ways, the ongoing and complicated web of problems in Haiti has been further entangled by misguided efforts to intervene.

It's very popular, for example, for American churches to donate a house, school, or church to a sister congregation. This is a great idea, especially considering that the earthquake leveled so many buildings. But too often, a U.S.-based group will raise funds for the building, hire a U.S.-based architect to design it, and then bring down its own members to do the construction. This approach fails to maximize the impact of the group's efforts. If that same U.S. church had hired a Haitian architect and builders, it would have helped a group of Haitians expand their skills and earn an income—while still raising a new building for the community. That same U.S. church could have then further helped stimulate the Haitian economy by planning a trip to visit the new sister church, and asking every traveler to bring an empty suitcase to fill with Haitian-made goods bought on the island.

Even the donation of goods can be a less-than-ideal intervention. Donations of emergency medicine and food during famine are critical, of course. But sending used consumer products that could easily be bought on-island undercuts the local economy. It would be more helpful to raise funds to buy sporting equipment, say, or shoes, from local sellers, ideally on an ongoing basis, which would provide consistent income for these merchants.

I would never criticize the spirit to serve others, and as a person so guided by my faith myself, I absolutely understand the call of these faith-based efforts. They're so important, and these missionaries and aid workers have the purest of intentions. But we all need to think hard about the *how* of giving and the ongoing impact.

TURNING TRASH INTO TREASURE AT PAPILLON

On our third day in Haiti, we went to Papillon, the artisan cooperative focused on orphan prevention that I'd visited on my first trip to the country. We've probably all read about how children in group homes often don't get enough human touch, and another popular service-related activity is visiting orphanages to hold babies as a way to help. It's a noble desire, but many of the orphans in Haiti have living parents who have given them up due to crippling poverty—a root cause that Papillon works to address.

Papillon primarily employs parents who have had serious economic hardship, and might send their children to a group home due to an inability to feed and house them, and ongoing messaging in Haiti suggesting that living in an orphanage with regular meals is better than staying home and going hungry. Some of these parents were never taught to read or write. Others have been deported from the United States, where they lived most of their lives, and have no family, connections, or jobs in Haiti. Papillon offers invaluable hope and job training to these parents and their families, and teaches them skills to create accessories, bags, and housewares from an amazing array of discarded items—oil drums, cardboard boxes, Haitian clay, pretty much anything they can find. Buying from Papillon is a way to support existing family units.

Papillon is an impressive operation, and it's grown hugely since it started ten years ago. It occupies an old limestone mansion, the walls painted in bright Caribbean colors. When we visited, artisans were at work in the open-air workshops throughout the house and on the grounds. There was a great, buzzy vibe. Some people were drilling down into their work. Others were chatting over the radio, which played a seemingly random mix of the 1990s and 2000s, with contemporary American Christian music thrown in. The atmosphere reminded me of a co-working space, maybe a Caribbean WeWork with the sun streaming in through the open roofs (and the occasional rain shower).

Papillon is a popular stop for mission groups, and visitors are often around. There's also a new childcare center for children of employees, and I heard the occasional sound of a child calling out or a couple of kids laughing. There are rooms for computer classes and language and literacy development. There's also a store selling handmade goods from Papillon and from other Haitian designers, a way to support the work taking place around the island. I saw sweet-looking stuffed animals, useful makeup pouches, and upcycled cardboard jewelry.

The last time I visited Papillon, I'd been particularly struck by the beads that some of the artisans were rolling from cardboard soda cases. It seemed amazing that the beads came from trash—old boxes that most of us toss without a thought—and I'd sent photos of the work to General Mills, explaining that the bright colors of cereal boxes would create a particularly interesting aesthetic. I added that ordering jewelry made from these beads would let them display their commitment to recycling in a creative way. General Mills makes popular cereals including Cocoa Puffs, Lucky Charms, and (my personal favorite) Honey Nut Cheerios. General Mills has more than one hundred food brands, sold in more than one hundred countries, and offers eight natural and organic lines. The company has become a leader in sustainable practices, and sits high on *Newsweek*'s green rankings.

General Mills loved the ingenuity of the idea, and the results. The company ultimately ordered two hundred bracelets and two hundred necklaces strung from cereal box beads to give as gifts to parenting bloggers and social media influencers for Mother's Day 2017. This was thousands of dollars' worth of jewelry, a pretty big order for this co-op, and for us. The order had employed twenty-five people at Papillon, from the cutters to the rollers to the shippers, generating a living wage (which is three times the minimum wage in Haiti), and giving them access to Papillon's medical and social benefits.

Back in the United States, the upcycled jewelry had really gotten influencers talking. I love collaborating with companies on great products for gifting and marketing. They make such a compelling story, and sometimes the social media influencers include a mention of To the Market in their posts. Most large companies today are looking for influencer gifts in addition to doing more traditional advertising. Influencer campaigns allow for social media personalities to post and share personal stories about their experience with the brand. For example, a parenting blogger likely wouldn't be compelled to share a photo captioned: "Here I am, eating cereal!" But if she receives a great gift with a good story, she can write: "Look what General Mills sent me! It's made from cereal boxes in Haiti. Thank you, General Mills, for supporting parents!"

I'm also a big fan of products like the cereal box bead bracelets because they create such surprise and delight when people learn about their origin. Upcycling in general can be a good reminder to value what we have—not only our objects but also our experiences and relationships. Repurposing sheds light on our existing good fortune. I see it as a way to honor ourselves, our past, the products we've already bought, and the decisions we've already made.

I'm always looking for ways to "upcycle" To the Market's existing relationships, and to build on the connections and successful partnerships we've already initiated. Too often in business, we think that to expand our client base or to invigorate a program, team, or line, we need to do something totally new, start from scratch, trash the old ways and innovate. But this "always new" mentality can mean overlooking what we've already invested in, and missing out on the value readily available to us in our existing product lines, people, or skill sets. This time, on my second visit to Papillon, I noticed a worker in a bright red Papillon T-shirt and chin-length dreadlocks sitting at a table, smiling as he folded cardboard strips into narrow ribbons. He then rolled the ribbons into disks that he shaped into butterflies and stars that could be hung like ornaments. Perhaps General Mills would want to do a holiday marketing campaign with cereal box ornaments? I snapped some photos and made a mental note to pitch the team there again.

ORPHANHOOD IN HAITI: A CLOSER LOOK AT THE PROBLEM

Papillon was started by Shelley Jean, an American woman who wanted to adopt a child and flew down to Haiti in 2007 with the intention of doing so. During that week-long trip to Haiti, she found herself rocked by the realization that there were thousands of kids in often-derelict orphanages who had living parents.

"They'd come to the orphanage to visit their children," she says. "I had this total paradigm shift—it suddenly wasn't about me wanting to adopt, but about these poor mothers who couldn't afford to feed their children and wound up giving them away. I was already a mother of two and I could not imagine being in a place where I would give my children away because I couldn't feed them."

Jean went home and created a nonprofit called the Apparent Project to help Haitian parents build job skills and also life skills such as financial literacy. Nine months later, she and her family moved to Haiti to get it going on the ground there. Jean spent a year living as a house parent in an orphanage and learning Creole. "I was thinking maybe I'd help two or three mothers," Jean says. Instead, through a series of stops and starts, she wound up creating Papillon.

UNICEF estimates that there were nearly 500,000 orphans in Haiti as of 2012—this in a country of about ten million people. Haiti also has kids living on the street, and others who work as house helpers. Called "restavek," these child house servants are essentially slaves. The United Nations and other groups consider the restavek to be victims of child trafficking. Various organizations are involved in trying to stop this practice, including the United Nations, Partners In Health, and the U.S. Department of State. Nonprofits such as Restavek Freedom are also trying to tackle this unique Haitian challenge.

Jean sees the problem of orphanhood in Haiti as having gotten worse over the years. Some Haitians have been lured into giving up their children for cash, sometimes to people who have set up absolutely inadequate facilities for childcare. There have been some truly heartbreaking accounts of what can happen to a child living in one of these places. We also now know the psychological damage that can happen when one child in a family is sent to a group home, even a good one, while his siblings remain with their parents. Most of the kids in these orphanages don't get adopted.

You can help reverse this trend by purchasing products made by parents through Papillon or another similar group. "It shouldn't be easier to check your child into an orphanage than it is to get a job," says Jean.

You can also support malnutrition clinics for children, maternity care and midwifery facilities, and skills-training centers for parents. Or cover a child's tuition or contribute money to a school. (But do your research and make sure it's a good school.)

As Jean puts it, "If you want to help, it's really important to take the time to really look and listen before jumping in and trying to *do*. We don't know the nuances of these different cultures, and there's a reason behind everything they do. Coming from a non-poverty mind-set, we need to work to understand the reasons before trying to change behavior."

The next day, we headed to Atelier Calla, where I could finally see how the earrings I'd designed came out. Christelle Paul had relocated her workshop to a new spot because the old neighborhood had become too dangerous. The new place, still in Port-au-Prince, was surrounded by a concrete wall (of course) and accessed through a metal gate.

We parked out front and walked through the gate to find a small, intimate indoor/outdoor studio and office, with samples all around.

There were about five men working with horn that day, which is really labor intensive, and they sat with their heads down, focused on what they were doing. I could hear hammering coming from somewhere else in the courtyard, as well as sanding and sawing. About four dozen cow horns sat in a pile on the ground, black and dusty. Paul had gotten the horns from local butchers and people who travel around the island to collect them. The horns were short and curved, hollow at one end and tapering to a closed point at the other.

We watched a man with short, slightly graying hair soften the horns. He sat on a low, ladder-backed cane chair in front of a copper cookstove filled with charcoal briquettes. He was wearing khaki shorts and a tank top, and he rested one arm on his knee while stirring two horns around in the coals with a big wooden stick. It looked like he was making horn stew, or maybe blackening horn sausages. At one point, he removed the heated horns from the fire and immediately placed them in a metal press sitting near his feet. He spun a wheel to drop a top plate, flattening the horns. He quickly tossed two more horns on the coals. It was amazing to see just how much work it took for this rough material to be transformed into sheets thin enough to cut.

In another spot, a couple of men were sawing boards of reddish, warm-hued obeche wood into smaller pieces, then wrapping them in pairs with twine. The men wore dust masks, and one sat on a wrought-iron patio chair, its white paint chipping. The chairs looked like what you'd expect to find in the courtyard of a fancy hotel. They were similar, in fact, to the chairs on the slate-floored, bougainvillea-lined patio at the Hotel Montana, where we were staying again.

I noticed a new product that Paul had lying on a table outside—brooches with intricate beading work. This beading was done by another group, Paul said. I asked if she could make some adjustments

HOP ON OVER TO HAITI FOR AN "EMPOWERMENT TOUR"

A beautiful, underappreciated country with a community-oriented spirit, Haiti feels much farther away than it is. As Callie Himsl, an American who works at Papillon, puts it, "It feels more like Africa than the Caribbean." For your next tropical vacation, instead of lying on the beach for a week, consider a seven-day "empowerment tour" organized by Papillon. The trip is super fun, safe, and can be life-changing.

You'll join a half-dozen other travelers to start your trip with a day at Papillon. You'll learn to make beaded bracelets in the morning, have lunch at the café, then throw clay on the wheel in the afternoon. You also can talk to the artisans about their lives, which, as Himsl says, lets you move past the image you may have of "flies on babies and trash on the streets." You meet real mothers and fathers, and establish personal connections.

During the week, you'll visit the Haiti Design Co-op, another artisan-based social enterprise, see the metal market in Croix-des-Bouquets, tour a few other successful co-ops, and spend a day at the beach.

Papillon organizes the entire thing, including meals, transportation, and lodging. You stay at a guesthouse or with a family, usually an employee of Papillon. "Living with someone lets you talk about your day," says Himsl, who often hosts visitors in her home. "You can sit on the balcony at night, and work through the emotions. Any time you travel to the third world there's a lot of emotions.

"Our hope is that people will come down with an empty suitcase or two and fill it up with things they buy on their trip. Then go back and tell people how beautiful these places are!"

to the design for our clients. She agreed to make samples and to drop them off at our hotel before we left.

It was great to witness all this activity, but I was most eager to see the samples of the cow horn earrings. Would they have the high-end look I'd envisioned? Could we translate horn into something finished and fashion forward?

We stepped into Paul's tiny, makeshift office, decorated with samples of brands ranging from Donna Karan to local Haitian designers. She handed me a paper bag containing two pairs of each of the four styles I'd requested. I spread them out on my palm. They looked even better than I could have imagined. She hadn't made major changes to the design, but she'd tweaked my concepts to make the most of the material. One pair of drop earrings had three oval disks in three different colors of horn—gray, cream, and tan. The proportions were perfect, and I loved her choice of colors and how each of the ovals had a slightly different shape. Her artisans had managed to press the horns thin enough to be lightweight, cut them with very precise, clean edges, and sand them into an amazing glass-like sheen. They'd connected the disks with fat gold rings that elevated the aesthetic and made the earrings look more expensive, and chosen high-end posts of surgical steel.

These earrings were exactly what I'd hoped to see made after my conversation with Nate. They could easily fit in at a Saks Fifth Avenue, Neiman Marcus, or Bloomingdale's, yet they were made from discarded cow horn that started as a dusty remain on a floor in Haiti. It was amazing to see such humble raw materials transformed through creativity (and muscle power) into objects of such beauty.

Paul talked a little about her journey into artisanship. She'd been a banker in Haiti, it turned out, before becoming a designer. But she'd always had a creative side. She was attracted to the horn material and started experimenting with it. People responded to her designs, leading her to eventually open a workshop.

I wasn't surprised to learn that she was a self-taught designer who hadn't planned to work with artisans. Everywhere I've gone on this journey to start my company, I've met truly amazing, inspiring people, most of whom stumbled into the sector. Many people, including myself, never imagined that they would be designing or selling products. Some people entered the artisan industry as a way to improve lives. Others, like Paul, were drawn by the materials and the process. It's an industry filled with people of very mixed education and experience, which makes it fascinating and also challenging. A lot of people, including myself, have to figure it out as they go along.

After Atelier Calla, we continued on to Croix-des-Bouquets, the town known for its metalwork. We picked up some samples of holiday ornaments made from upcycled oil drums that we'd ordered. They looked incredible, the steel cut into a holiday shape and hand-embossed with a raised pattern. We'd ordered doves, angels, fir trees, snowflakes, snowmen, and intricate crosses. We'd asked the artisans to apply a matte white paint on some, and gold leaf on others. They looked like ceramic pieces. It was another example of pushing the design and the material further than one would think possible.

Metal, which is so clearly useful, is still dumped into landfills at an alarming rate. In one of the many workshops that line the main drag of Croix-des-Bouquets, we saw artisans sitting on the ground in shorts and T-shirts, pounding steel with hammers, turning oil drums into wall art. It looked like back-breaking work. So many of the products we enjoy are extremely labor intensive, something this visit really drove home once again.

On our way to the airport, we had a little extra time, and I asked our guide, Samson, to show us another cooperative in Port-au-Prince. He suggested a local soap maker, which sounded exciting—my company wasn't yet carrying soap. We arrived at the workshop and found what looked like an abandoned building with expensive equipment sitting dormant. No one was working. It was like a hollowed-out version of the vibrant workshops I'd toured earlier. It was eerie, like seeing the shadow of a project. Someone had bought professional equipment, including the expensive metal vats needed for soap production. There'd been some real investment, but also obviously a disconnect somewhere that led to the business floundering.

There was one woman present who showed us around. The co-op had manufactured soap for a few local hotels, she told me, but had received no orders in the past six months. This was the first time I'd visited a workshop associated with the Artisan Business Network that didn't operate consistently.

We stopped in a room to look at samples. Perhaps the problem was the packaging, I thought. Unattractive Saran wrap–like plastic was stretched over each bar of soap, affixed with a poorly printed sticker. Or maybe the pricing was the problem; the soap was listed at a price far above the market rate for similar goods.

I walked back and forth in the sample room, picking up different designs and scents, turning them over, smelling them, trying to figure out if there was any "in" for us, any way we might work with this cooperative. But there was too much uncertainty for me to place an order. It was incredibly frustrating and sad to see so much effort gone to waste. I asked Samson what the women do when they're not making soap, and he said they sit at home.

The soap factory highlighted how vulnerable all these groups are—the moms and dads at Papillon, Paul's Atelier Calla, the men hammering metal in Croix-des-Bouquets. They're subject to the effectiveness of their leadership, to their ability to get their products seen, and to the whims of ever-changing consumer habits. They have to depend on their own good health and hardiness and consistent application. The entire country is fragile, despite all the color and industriousness and laughter I'd seen.

We left the factory and headed to the airport. That empty, hollow feeling lingered with me. It felt like a moment of reckoning. The fact is, my vision of using economic approaches to address social problems isn't guaranteed to help all the people involved either. We want to believe we have *the* perfect solution, and that while other approaches didn't work, ours will. But there's no guarantee that any of these projects will necessarily succeed. The private sector isn't a surefire solution to solving the chaos caused by poverty, environmental degradation, war, lack of education, or lack of respect for women and human life in general. Whatever approach we take, we must give serious and ongoing thought to the real sustainability of our vision.

The soap factory visit also highlighted the critical role of people like Sarah Lance, Nathalie Tancrede, and Christelle Paul, social-purpose visionaries who have committed their lives to leading these groups and working with them on a day-to-day basis. They're "middlewomen" of a sort, a word that can have negative connotations. But these middlewomen working on the ground with ethical producers—particularly artisans—are so important. They're the ones who communicate between very different worlds, balancing the demands of first-world commerce with the needs and challenges of those living in poverty and uncertainty. These people bridge many divides as they work to help create and sustain employment. I see them as translators of human potential. It's such a critical job, requiring real dynamism, perseverance, and vision. Leaving Haiti, I felt honored, once again, to have met so many of these heroes, and to see the success stories they've helped write.

FROM BONEYARD TO BESTSELLER

I returned home, eager to include the four different styles of cow horn earrings in our fall/winter 2017 collection. They quickly became bestsellers. We ended up having to do several rush reorders to keep up with the demand, which Paul was able to turn around quickly and consistently. Customers were ordering them from our site and even writing to ask when they'd arrive.

At one point, the sister of my friend Maggie saw someone wearing the horn earrings and asked where she could get them. She didn't realize that they were created by my company. I was thrilled to hear about this request. The earrings were selling themselves, proof that recycled materials can compete on the merits of their own design.

Later that year, I had the chance to meet Chris Wilkes, who runs Hearst's new entrepreneurship program, called HearstLab. Hearst Communications is a leading tastemaker that publishes major titles including *Elle*, *Harper's Bazaar*, *Marie Claire*, *Esquire*, *House Beautiful*, and *O, The Oprah Magazine*. I explained our mission and vision to Wilkes. He got excited about the possibility of having To the Market do holiday gifts for the friends and mentors of the entrepreneurship program.

Wilkes connected me to Judith Bookbinder, Hearst's vice president of creative communications. Bookbinder is a "super creative," responsible for making many of the corporation's design decisions.

She has been in the design and fashion world for decades, and has exquisite taste. I wore a pair of the cow horn earrings to our meeting in New York, and she loved them. I also showed her the little upcycled cow horn bowls in our catalog. She decided that the cow horn bowls would be perfect gifts for the entrepreneurship lab to give. Here was a top influencer of a major media powerhouse choosing recycled products to give under the Hearst brand. This model of social change does work, especially with people like Christelle Paul running professional operations, executing sophisticated designs, and bringing a unique skill set to the products.

I had set myself the challenge to design deeper, and I'd succeeded. Nate would love this story.

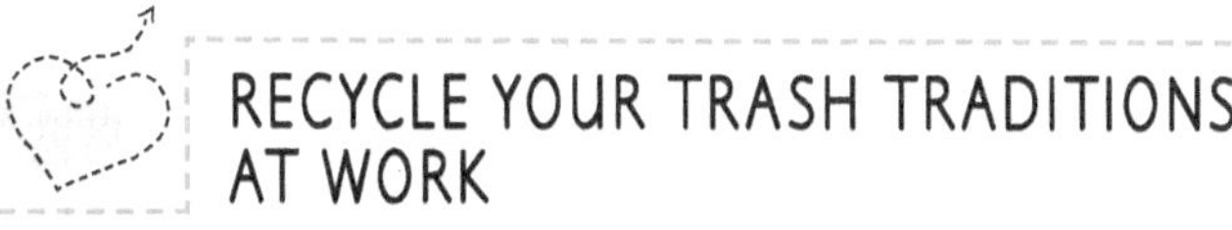

RECYCLE YOUR TRASH TRADITIONS AT WORK

No one wants more trash in landfills (except maybe landfill owners), but figuring out how to recycle or compost can take some effort. Fortunately, there are many ways to get involved with reducing trash at the office.

Use a Good Trash Hauler: Look at the logos on the trash trucks outside your building, or check your city's website to see who's hauling your garbage. Then investigate the company to see if it recycles. If not, look for an alternative hauler in your area that does (or contact a third party like Rubicon for suggestions). If you're a tenant in a large office building, make a case to the management about the importance of environmentally friendly waste removal, and suggest specific alternatives.

Go Green on Office Supplies: Replace plastic cups in the kitchen with reusable mugs—a great chance to add the company logo. Choose recycled paper products for printing, mailing, and shipping; New Leaf Paper is a leader in sustainable paper printing products. Order custom products made of recycled or organic materials and fabrics.

Put the Pause on Printing Waste: Default to double-sided printing for all in-office communications, use the backside of old printouts for draft documents and notes, and skip printing out emails.

Invite Customers to Contribute: Follow other fashion leaders. If you work at or own a retail store, put a receptacle by the door for empty containers of products you sell. The bath and body company Kiehl's, for example, has recycling bins for empty Kiehl's plastic bottles, cardboard packaging, and caps at all their U.S. stores. Customers get a point for every returned item; ten points earns a free, travel-size product. Kiehl's sends the material to TerraCycle, which makes cute accessories from hard-to-recycle materials, including coffee capsules, Capri Sun and chip bags, ink pens, and billboards. You can create an account with TerraCycle to participate in their free recycling programs. H&M recycles and donates used clothing from any brand; the company estimates that up to 95 percent of clothing that gets tossed could be recycled or even reworn. Men's Wearhouse donates gently used suits to men transitioning to self-sufficiency. Most Nike and Converse stores accept old athletic shoes too worn-out to be donated and ships them off, along with factory scraps, to be transformed into Nike Grind, a material used to create athletic tracks and playground surfaces. Eileen Fisher accepts worn-out clothing at its stores, which it resells or recycles. (Old jeans make cute new pouches.) Austin-based, award-winning Tèo gelato takes back its plastic containers (licked clean) and gives customers a free gelato for their effort.

Join the Zero Waste Movement: Check out the U.S. Zero Waste Business Council's resource section and ask your company to join.

Party with Purpose: The benefit corporation Preserve makes colorful, compostable straws, paper and plastic plates, and cutlery. Save leftover cake in the 100 percent recycled plastic food storage containers. Online store Geese and Ganders carries wooden utensils as an alternative to plastics as a part of its curated party supplies assortment.

Spearhead a Recycling Program at Your Office: Figure out what can be recycled in your zip code by looking online, then make it easy for fellow employees to follow along by putting out labeled bins. Recycle Across America offers inexpensive universal recycling signage—basically traffic signs for trash—that you may have seen at Bank of America, Macy's, or Whole Foods.

Think Partnership: Atlanta's football team, the Falcons, recently did an amazing partnership with Novelis, the world's largest aluminum recycler, and the Arthur M. Blank Family Foundation to collect empty aluminum cans from fans attending games at the stadium. The money earned from recycling and reselling the aluminum helped fund a Habitat for Humanity house near the stadium.

Tone Down Your Toner Waste: American businesses toss about one million toner cartridges every single day, a half billion ending up in landfills every year. It takes a single cartridge up to one thousand years to biodegrade. Many manufacturers now participate in office-based toner-cartridge recycling; your office can follow suit. Work at home? OfficeMax and Office Depot will take back empty toner cartridges from any manufacturer, bought at any store. Everycartridge.com provides a consumer-focused list of manufacturers' return programs.

CHAPTER FIVE

NOT ALL FACTORIES ARE EQUAL, OR EVIL

Line Production Done Well

You can design and create . . .
but it takes people to make the dream a reality.

—WALT DISNEY, AMERICAN ENTREPRENEUR

In early summer of 2017, I visited a denim factory in Nicaragua, where I tried my hand at sewing a pair of Wrangler jeans. I was seated on a little backless operator stool in a big, air-conditioned room, an industrial sewing machine on a metal arm between my knees. I was wearing jeans myself, as I often am, and a flowered blouse with bell sleeves—it was June in the Caribbean and sweltering outside. I had a pair of giant safety goggles strapped over my face and sat hunched over the machine with a hunk of denim in hand, ready to make some jeans . . . which I absolutely could not do.

Denim is surprisingly stiff and thick! I was totally incapable of sewing two pieces together in a straight line. I'd worked on a sewing machine in the past and assumed this experience would be similar, that the denim would feed smoothly under the needle. This was not the case. My sewing would never pass quality control; it was like a child trying to draw a masterpiece with crayons. My hair was loose and kept falling in front of my face, complicating matters. The operator whose stool I'd borrowed was assisting me and laughing nonstop, apparently having the time of his life watching this pathetic American woman attempting to do his job and failing miserably.

I was laughing pretty hard, too. It was fun to try to create something I always wear but have never seen made. It was as if I'd stepped into a kitchen for the first time to bake bread after having eaten it my whole life, and wound up with a doughy mess. We've all worn jeans, most of us for decades (some of us rarely wear anything else). Yet we've never tried to make them, let alone given much thought to how they're constructed.

In another section of the factory, workers created that on-trend, "distressed" look, which isn't just printed on denim, it turns out. Men manually sand the jeans, slipping one pair after the next onto horizontal mannequin legs, and running a hand sander back and forth. The workers had the attitude of craftsmen, trying to achieve exactly the right well-worn look—faded around the knees and at the hips. They were using a huge amount of physical effort, as if they were in an all-day rowing competition. I was shocked to see how much work went into the jeans.

Seeing firsthand the labor and sheer skill involved in making these clothes was an important lesson for me. We've lost the connection between what we buy and who made it, in many regards. We don't see our mass-produced products being made, and the level of quality and uniformity at factories today can make it easy to forget that real people work there, that someone's day was spent making those jeans or shoes or mugs. When you buy a unique handicraft made by artisans, the irregular look may make you reflect on the fact that those beads were rolled by hand. But some of the products we buy today from factories are so perfect and sometimes so affordable that it's easy to assume they were manufactured by a robot.

For most of human history, clothing was made by hand for a specific person. If we'd been born a hundred years ago, we'd each have only a handful of items, all sewn by our own mother or by a seamstress down the street, whom we perhaps also saw every Sunday in church. Our makers were close to us, literally and figuratively. Today, the average American buys something like seventy pieces of clothing a year. Between the years 2000 and 2014, the number of garments the average consumer bought increased by 60 percent. I can't imagine what someone living in the 1800s or mid-1900s would think about the piles of sweaters, T-shirts, workout pants, and jeans most of us have crammed into our drawers, or the dozens of dresses, blouses, jackets, and coats dripping from hangers in our closets.

When thinking about the rise of mass production, most people point to the aha moment of Henry Ford, who brought the efficiency of assembly-line production to car manufacturing in Detroit in 1914. But clothing factories and fabric mills had been operating in England since the mid-1800s, often employing workers, including children, who were subject to punishingly long hours and unsafe conditions. The Industrial Revolution that kicked off in the mid-1700s brought with it faster, more efficient ways to spin cotton into thread, and then to sew fabric into clothing. After the sewing machine was invented in the mid-1800s, mass production of clothing really took off, and has been accelerating ever since.

In the United States, the "rag trade" became a major employer in New York City's Lower East Side by the turn of the twentieth century, with young immigrant women laboring in sweatshops, often in utterly deplorable conditions. In the 1900s, when our industrial age took off, there were truly dangerous practices and plenty of cases of labor exploitation here.

The most infamous accident in a U.S. sweatshop occurred at the

Triangle Shirtwaist Company factory in New York City in 1911. The company had sweatshops on the eighth, ninth, and tenth floors of a factory building on the Lower East Side. The factory owners had been warned about the risk of fire but had not made changes. The factory employed mostly young women, immigrants who'd fled poverty and religious persecution in Russia, or who'd come to the United States from Italy. They sat hunched over sewing machines in the cramped, crowded building, working six days a week sewing "shirtwaists," or ladies' blouses. For immigrants in NYC, particularly those in the process of learning English, working in garment factories was often the best option.

When a fire broke out on March 25, 1911, it quickly ignited the fabric scraps lying around. The fabric burst into flames. The women scrambled for the exits. Some women were able to escape by the stairs or the elevators, until smoke and fire made these unusable. But the door to one of the main exits was locked, reportedly a common practice in factories at the time to discourage workers from slipping out for a break or stealing.

About twenty women crowded onto a single fire escape one hundred feet above the sidewalk. But the fire escape was insecurely attached and eventually collapsed, plunging the workers to the sidewalk and killing them. Other girls jumped out of windows to their death. Some hid in stockrooms and died by asphyxiation or burning.

When the firefighters arrived, their ladders weren't long enough to reach people, and their nets ripped under the weight of those who jumped. By the time the fire was out, 146 people had died, the vast majority women, some as young as fourteen. This was the worst industrial accident in New York City and one of the worst in the United States. This incident put new focus on labor conditions at factories here and led to real changes in workplace safety.

In New York, a committee on safety was formed, led by Frances Perkins, who had been an eyewitness to the fire (and was appointed United States secretary of labor two decades later). This committee identified problems and led to the creation of the Factory Investigating Commission, which conducted exhaustive research at facilities around the state. The factory investigating commission ultimately led to dozens of new laws being passed in New York state, and eventually nationally, including everything from requiring fire extinguishers and fire sprinklers in buildings, to constructing bathroom facilities for workers, to drafting labor laws to protect women and children. Labor unions also began forming and strengthening, including the International Ladies' Garment Workers Union, which fought for more improvements.

Shortly after, American factories began ramping up production, turning their attention to manufacturing wartime necessities. In World War II, production increased again. The contribution of weapons made in U.S. factories was a decisive factor in both world wars. I read so much about military strategy in high school and college, and I was amazed to learn that the munitions industry in the United States was staffed by a significant number of women, many of whom stepped into traditionally male roles after the men went off to fight. The "We Can Do It" image of Rosie the Riveter, wearing a red kerchief and a work shirt with rolled-up sleeves, is a lasting visual reminder of women's efforts in factories during World War II.

After World War II, these factories kept working, but they switched to churning out consumer goods. There are a handful of famous pop cultural references to this rise of mechanization. My favorite is the classic *I Love Lucy* episode called "Job Switching," from 1952. Lucy and Ethel get jobs in a candy factory to prove a point about their competence to Ricky and Fred. At first, they calmly wrap up each piece of chocolate as it passes by on the conveyor belt. Then the belt starts moving faster. Lucy and Ethel can't keep up. They begin popping chocolates into their mouths and sweeping chocolates into their factory-supplied hats. Lucy dumps chocolates down the front of her dress. The manager, seeing their "success," increases the conveyor belt speed. Chocolate chaos ensues.

Many economists look at the increase in mass production as intrinsically tied to the rise of the American middle class. As mass production grew in the United States, the cost of consumer goods fell. Many people could now stock up on clothing, shoes, and appliances—the kinds of nonessential products formerly reserved for the rich. Factory workers began to have enough income to buy single-family houses in the comfortable suburbs that grew around cities; foremen, managers, and executives could spring for even larger spreads.

American companies also began operating factories abroad, generally in countries that used high tariffs and quotas to block American imports such as toothpaste and cars. Overseas factories also allowed companies to easily tweak products for specific markets and access raw materials that were abundant on the ground. By the 1980s, this trend of manufacturing and selling overseas to tap into the wealth of non-U.S. consumers had really accelerated, specifically in Europe and Asia. As Oren Shaffer, then chief financial officer at the Goodyear Tire and Rubber Company, told the *New York Times* in 1989, "If you really want to be a player, you have to be inside foreign markets. You can't export."

But U.S. companies also began doing something else that troubled some industry analysts—and increasingly, U.S. workers: manufacturing overseas with cheaper labor and then shipping products back to sell to consumers here. Debates raged about the economic and social good of offshore production, and continue today. Regardless of how you feel about offshoring, one clear result is that the majority of the products we buy and use are made by people living very far away. Only about 15 percent of apparel is manufactured in the United States, North and South America, and the Caribbean.

To those of us who love fashion and care about ethical sourcing, one important issue remains unchanged, regardless of where clothing is made. Factories provide real jobs for real people, and we need to pay attention to the conditions in which they work.

THE RISE AND FALL (AND RELOCATION) OF THE BIG, BAD FACTORY

When you look at the low cost of some of the items available to us today, it's hard to imagine how these prices can exist without labor exploitation. How could such an inexpensive, super-soft T-shirt get made and tagged and shipped without someone, somewhere, going to bed hungry? How can a "fast fashion" brand offer its dresses and down jackets and leggings at such low prices? Fast fashion has been a particularly hot segment of the industry lately, with compressed production cycles turning out up-to-the-minute designs, and consumers treating their lowest-priced garments as nearly disposable, discarding them after just seven or eight wears. We're keeping clothes about half as long as we did only fifteen years ago. Were these inexpensive items really produced in a way that means we can wear them with a comfortable conscience?

It turns out that line production, in and of itself, needn't be dehumanizing, dangerous, or environmentally destructive. There are business strategies that can lead to even very low prices, while employing workers in decent conditions at a fair wage. Brands like Old Navy can reap major cost savings through bulk purchases of fabric and trims, such as zippers. You might not think that purchasing at a large scale would make that much of a difference, but fabric suppliers set prices based on the amount you buy, as does everyone else. At To the Market, we procure fabric for some of our cut-and-sew producers, and reams of cotton will literally cost us half when we double our order—and our orders are nowhere near the size of Old Navy (yet!).

Clothing can also drop in price when a company makes more units of fewer designs. A limited number of styles means fewer samples need to be made, which cuts costs and allows for manufacturing efficiencies, such as operators learning the construction or detailing only once and then producing at greater speeds.

These are efficient ways to cut costs ethically, but low prices can also be tied to deplorable working conditions—cost savings made on the labor side in a way that leads to serious human rights challenges. Sometimes workers have no other choice but to take a job that may endanger their lives. The employees may be poor and uneducated, living in remote areas with few options, eager for any kind of work and willing to accept low wages and poor conditions.

Factories as a whole can be critical parts of the growth of many developing nations, providing the only real economic opportunity. A community's life may revolve around the factory (or field). In Uzbekistan, schools will shut down so kids can pick cotton. In the United States today, a city would never interrupt education to send fifth graders to work in the fields, but for some communities struggling with daily survival, economic opportunity comes before education or even safe working conditions. A colleague from the International Labour Organization (ILO) told me, frankly, that that ILO doesn't advocate for shutting down bad factories, for fear of leaving operators (the

A NEW LIFE FOR OLD CLOTHES

Clothing is one of the easiest items to upcycle. A gently used item of yours can be a huge asset to someone else, especially for a special occasion that requires a high-cost outfit. Check out these category-specific ways to donate:

Dress for Success: Preparing for a job interview can take a lot of thought. Worrying about the affordability of an appropriate interview outfit shouldn't be an additional burden. So goes the thinking of this international nonprofit that provides professional attire for vulnerable women seeking employment. The nonprofit also offers life-skills training and a support system to help women move toward economic independence. Local affiliates accept gently used clothing and accessories and unused beauty products.

Becca's Closet: In high school, Rebecca Kirtman decided to collect hundreds of prom dresses to donate to girls in South Florida who might otherwise skip the dance due to the high cost of the dress. A year later, while still in high school, this budding humanitarian was killed in a car accident. Her family, along with friends and strangers, started Becca's Closet in her memory. Becca's Closet awards "dress scholarships" to high school seniors who have shown leadership in their communities. You can donate your gently used dresses by finding your local Becca's Closet chapter.

Brides Across America: This nonprofit helps military brides, many of whom are living on a small salary, feel like Cinderella on their wedding day by giving them beautiful (used) wedding gowns. To donate your dress (and wedding accessories, such as a veil), fill out the application form online.

Once Upon A Child: Once Upon A Child is the largest U.S. resale franchise that buys and sells gently used kids' and baby clothing and gear, helping moms in two ways: by selling safe, clean products at a good price and by offering parents the opportunity to recycle children's nearly new items and get paid on the spot.

Out of the Closet: This nonprofit with thrift stores in more than a dozen cities donates 96¢ from every dollar to fund AIDS Healthcare Foundation's HIV/AIDS programs and services.

industry term for factory workers) without income. Instead, the ILO—like many big brands—focuses on remediation, helping a factory make incremental improvements and allowing the workers to keep earning in the meantime.

Buyers can put serious pressure on factory owners and managers, driving down wages and limiting the time and money a manufacturer spends on improvements. Sometimes factory owners or managers focus on the bottom line to the exclusion of the employees, as if they are interchangeable widgets themselves. But well-meaning managers and factory owners can face a shortage of orders and a demand for lower prices from buyers, and be forced to decide between cutting wages and cutting employees. Either decision has bad consequences for workers. As Marsha Dickson, a professor of fashion and apparel studies at the University of Delaware, recently told the *South China Morning Post*, "What we have seen over many years is that a manufacturer's ability to use sustainable methods, provide good working conditions, better pay, fewer hours, and so on is greatly affected by the relationship it has with its buyers."

As consumers, we, too, can aggravate price pressure. We all love a bargain, but this desire for a good deal, if combined with a blind eye to working conditions, can translate into clothing that's been manufactured and sold at a low price that is, in fact, too good to be true.

I assumed that labor exploitation was more likely in a large factory setting than in a small cooperative or business because the sheer scale of the facility would make it hard to catch. With thousands of people coming and going, often on two or even three shifts, I was certain it would be harder for managers to keep tabs on the well-being of individual workers, or even to know their exact age. However, I came to learn that small factories face challenges, too. They don't always have the infrastructure or the capabilities to manage safety and welfare.

The fashion industry, particularly apparel manufacturing, also can put a huge strain on the environment. A garment involves many pieces and processes—growing raw materials, spinning and weaving, dying, cutting and sewing, shipping, selling, and even disposal. There are many places along this route where the process can damage the planet. Cotton, used in 40 percent of clothing, requires a huge amount of water to grow. It can take more than five thousand gallons of water to manufacture a T-shirt and a pair of jeans. Synthetic materials, meanwhile, can be huge polluters.

According to a United Nations 2017 World Water Development Report, more than 80 percent of the world's wastewater—including that of garment factories—is released into the environment without being treated. Communities near these facilities may be drinking, cooking, and bathing in tainted water, and local marine life may be poisoned. That wastewater, if treated, could be valuable for irrigation or other purposes. In the United States, some companies have moved away from environmentally harmful production practices at all their facilities, but others have merely moved the pollution offshore. As sustainable fashion pioneer Eileen Fisher has put it, "The clothing industry is the second-largest polluter in the world . . . second only to oil. It's a really nasty business . . . it's a mess."

In the United States, factory workers are largely protected by national and state regulations, as well as by the voluntary participation of companies in various certification programs. In 1970, Congress passed the national Occupational Safety and Health Act, which was then signed into law by President Nixon. This congressional act created the Occupational Safety and Health Administration, charged with setting and enforcing safe working conditions and providing training, outreach, education, and assistance. This national labor reform came on the heels of the outcry against rising injuries and deaths on the job.

But these laws don't apply in the developing world. Lack of safety regulations and/or the ability to enforce them can lead to truly heartbreaking conditions, and even the death of factory workers.

In November 2012, a fire broke out at a nine-story factory in the outskirts of Dhaka, the capital of Bangladesh, one of the world's largest garment producers. This was a facility where many U.S. and European companies had outsourced production. The fire caught on scrap material and spread throughout the building. It took firefighters seventeen hours to put it out. More than one hundred people died.

There was an outcry around the globe. Then, five months later, an even worse disaster struck in Bangladesh. The five-story Rana Plaza factory building in Dhaka collapsed in April 2013. As the building crumbled, more than one thousand workers were killed. Thousands more were injured. This was the worst garment factory disaster in known history. Many of the largest brands and retailers in the world outsourced garment production to workers in this factory—including plenty of popular companies we buy from in the United States.

The tragedy caused global outrage. Activists and students protested the lack of safety for workers. Media in the United States, Europe, and Asia began focusing more on factories. *The Guardian* newspaper in London began an online section called "Rana Plaza," focusing on ethical fashion. (The section continues to be an active forum for issues around ethical fashion today.)

THE GOOD FACTORY GOES GLOBAL

After the Rana Plaza disaster in Bangladesh, many fashion industry leaders took a harder look at their own supply chain, agreeing with the protesters that "no one should die for fashion." Two groups were established with this aim: the Accord on Fire and Building Safety in Bangladesh, which includes brands like Adidas, Abercrombie & Fitch, Vistaprint, and Inditex (owner of Zara); and the Alliance for Bangladesh Worker Safety, which includes Gap, Walmart, Target, and VF Corporation, a fashion conglomerate that owns some of the world's most recognized brands, including Vans, the North Face, Timberland, and Wrangler. Both the Alliance and the Accord are designed to address the health and safety of workers and provide opportunities for labor unions to have some measure of bargaining power in Bangladesh.

I had the opportunity to peek behind the curtain and see how jeans are made at a Wrangler factory because I'd recently been appointed to the new Responsible Sourcing Advisory Council at VF. While not involved in the Rana Plaza disaster, VF Corporation nonetheless decided to scale up its own work on supply-chain improvements after the accident. (VF does not own any factories in Bangladesh, but it contracts with approximately ninety factories there that employ nearly 200,000 workers.) VF created the council to gain insight into ways to improve the factories it sources from, not only in Bangladesh but also in the rest of the world.

I'd been invited to an initial meeting to learn about VF in Decem-

WHAT NOT TO WEAR
HOW TO CHECK SOURCING

How can you tell if that cute shirt or sweater was produced by a person earning a decent wage and working in a safe factory versus someone subject to dangerous and dehumanizing practices? Here are some ways to find out.

Search Sweat & Toil: This app, a comprehensive resource developed by the U.S. Department of Labor, highlights commodities in specific countries that often rely on child labor, such as cotton from Uzbekistan and seafood from Thailand. You can check categories of products you use, see where the greatest risks are, then investigate potentially offending products more deeply. You can also learn about countries' efforts to eliminate child labor.

See What the Brand Says: You can be a virtual Sherlock Holmes by checking company websites, which increasingly share a huge amount about sourcing practices, sustainability efforts, and other corporate social responsibility programs. The Gap, for example, has made "Gap for Good" a consistent message on its homepage, advertising the company's actions on a valuable (and expensive) e-commerce page. Publicly held companies are accountable to investors and the law, meaning they have a vested interest in making good on the actions they claim.

Browse for Benefit Corporations: You can seek suppliers making a positive impact on society and employees by looking for benefit corporations, which are for-profit companies focused on pro-social *and* economic goals. You can search by state and choose to buy from a benefit corporation whose products you love.

Check Sourcemap: This new technology allows companies to visually display the journey of products and their components on a map of the world. For example, a cotton tote bag made in New York may show its YKK zippers coming from a facility outside Atlanta, Georgia; the cotton coming from a producer in Punjab, India; and the cutting and sewing taking place in Brooklyn, New York. Brands can add information about each facility, stating who owns it, how big it is, and whether it has any certifications, such as fair trade.

ber of 2015. I walked in (wearing my black Vans), wondering what this $12 billion corporation was trying to do and what role I might play. I learned that VF was determined to avoid contracting with producers that weren't following strict environmental and social standards. VF also wanted to help factories it works with make important improvements in terms of worker well-being, workplace safety, environmental impact, and the use and disposal of chemicals. I was honored to be asked to be on the advisory council and to help with this aim.

In 2017, VF Corporation began inviting the members of the new council to tour factories. What I've learned from my time at VF and through my own research and travel is that not all factories are bad places to work—just as not all small producers or artisan cooperatives meet good social and environmental standards. A good factory meets the basic needs of operators, including safety, freedom of movement, adequate light and temperature control and ventilation, and decent wages. Safe conditions protect operators—and the factory. Fewer accidents mean fewer production delays, and less bad press that can drive away customers. Paying laborers a decent wage can mean healthier, happier, more loyal and more productive workers, and lower absentee and turnover rates. A company-supported health clinic means fewer days lost to illness.

The efforts by VF are great to see and are part of a larger trend toward U.S. labor reforms moving overseas. Today, many big brands have made public commitments to improve their supply chain.

Sometimes leaders in emerging economies push back against the demand for better labor laws, regulation, and environmental accountability. They may point out that successful Western economies were able to develop largely uninhibited by environmental or social constraints. It's true that many of our biggest brands in the United States were built before today's labor laws were put in place, and that American industries grew without interference from other countries insisting we improve our ways.

But the developing world is running factories in a new era, one with a far greater focus on human rights and environmental sustainability. Today, good working conditions and a minimal environmental footprint are increasingly essential to doing business, in part because today's growing supply-chain transparency means that bad behavior will be seen and punished by consumers and buyers who have a choice. Many companies will pull out of a country with rampant, unaddressed child labor or other exploitative practices. They might leave because their own corporate commitment to human rights clashes with the labor practices of a particular country or factory. Most major brands won't buy cotton from Uzbekistan, for example, because the risk of having child labor in the supply chain is too high. New regulations also make old-style labor exploitation increasingly risky for the factory owners from a legal standpoint.

At To the Market, we always want to partner with organizations that ensure workers have freedom of movement, fair payment, and safe working conditions, and that abide by legal age restrictions. When assessing a potential new producer, we look at who referred us and evaluate whether that person can act as a good reference. Then we ask the potential producer questions about the operation, and we go visit it ourselves, have someone else visit, or look at previous audit reports completed by brands we trust. We've had unfortunate instances of discovering that a cooperative is outsourcing part of its production to a factory with questionable working conditions or one that doesn't fit our mission of employing vulnerable communities. In these cases, we have to decline the chance to work with that producer.

Co-ops, for all the great work they do, generally can't employ the same large numbers of people as factories can—and people need jobs around the world. When factories treat workers well, pay attention to their environmental impact, and contribute to their communities, they provide regular employment and products we can feel good about buying. A nation absolutely *can* develop economically while respecting human rights. It's not only possible, but also increasingly necessary to remain competitive. Fair and just economic development is more humane *and* more sustainable than a system built on exploitation. When factories act as "good citizens," they are important, positive drivers of economic and social development.

ON THE GROUND IN A GOOD FACTORY

The New Hampshire–based footwear manufacturer Timberland is a classic American success story. In the late 1920s, a Ukrainian immigrant named Nathan Swartz began working as a shoe stitcher in his new hometown of Boston. By the 1950s, he'd managed to buy his own shoe store, and a few years later, he brought in his two sons to help. In the mid-sixties, this shoe-focused family introduced injection-molding technology, great for making waterproof footwear. This led to the introduction of the now-iconic waterproof yellow leather boot called Timberland. The boot was such a hit among New Englanders that the Swartz family changed the company's name to the Timberland Company and went on to add other styles.

Today, Timberland produces footwear in factories around the world, including a sixteen-building facility in the Dominican Republic. In 2011, the VF Corporation bought the Timberland Company, including the D.R. factory, which has been turning out boots for thirty-five years. Timberland D.R. is an example of a good factory, the kind of place where workers profess their loyalty, speak about the products with pride, and wear them. The acquisition by VF brought more resources to a factory that already had a focus on being a good citizen. "There's been a shift toward sustainability and employee well-being, a big thing for VF," says general manager Fernando Schneider, who was recruited from Brazil four years ago by VF to head up operations in the D.R. Schneider, who has forty years' experience in footwear, says that while it was a growing industry in Brazil, rising labor costs and a strong *real*, the Brazilian unit of currency, drove many factories to Asia. Working in the D.R. offered him the chance to take a good factory and make it even better, in part by including employees in the CSR aims.

The Timberland production facility in the D.R. sits in a cheery industrial park in Santiago, the second-largest city in this lush, hilly Caribbean country that shares the island of Hispaniola with Haiti. The Timberland campus resembles a factory outlet mall in the United States—long buildings branching off from paved roadways with grassy areas between. This park, however, contains *actual* factories (and no shoppers rushing around with their bags). The 3,300 workers currently employed here turn out 18,000 pairs of boots *a day*, or four million a year.

The office is in a two-story building with frosted-glass double doors, shiny tile floors, and a display of vintage sewing machines and shoe forms painted blue, aqua, yellow, and white. The air-conditioned reception area feels hip and on-brand; the receptionist is wearing a knit Timberland hat with snowflakes stitched around the perimeter (despite the palm trees and humid, eighty-plus-degree weather outside).

ALTERNATIVE FABRICS
OLD AND NEW ECO OPTIONS

Factories increasingly make clothing and accessories from a new breed of sustainable fabrics, many developed in response to the increasing consumer demand for eco-friendly materials. Check labels for these textile types:

Hemp: The plant is renewable, easy to harvest, and requires little to no pesticides to grow. Versatile hemp fabric can be used for soft goods like T-shirts and more structured items like bags. The manufacturing process doesn't require heavy chemicals, making it a favorite of brands including Patagonia, Eileen Fisher, AG Adriano Goldschmied, The Lost Explorer, and Duluth Trading Company.

Organic Cotton: Organic cotton is grown without pesticides, insecticides, or GMOs, making it good for the environment and for the farmers growing and picking it. Another safe bet for fairly farmed cotton is to buy fair trade certified or from a producer participating in the Better Cotton Initiative, a nonprofit focused on improving the environmental and labor standards of cotton harvesting. Levi's, Gap Inc., and VF Corporation all lead on sourcing cotton through the Better Cotton Initiative.

Pineapple Leather: Piñatex, a vegan leather alternative made of pineapple leaf fiber, is the brainchild of Dr. Carmen Hijosa, who pursued a PhD in her late fifties at the Royal College of Art in the UK. Pineapple leather is a natural, sustainable alternative that can be used in products ranging from automobiles to clothing to accessories.

Tencel: Tencel is a super-soft, biodegradable, rayon-like fabric made from the pulp of sustainable eucalyptus trees. You can find Tencel in pants, shirts, dresses, and more at the Gap.

The D.R. has seen huge economic development since the 1960s, after the cruel dictator, Rafael Trujillo, was assassinated in 1961. While the economy of neighboring Haiti continues to languish, the Dominican Republic grew throughout the latter half of the twentieth century and has experienced an almost meteoric rise in GDP since 2000. The D.R.'s GDP, a number that describes the economic value of all the goods and services produced within a country, is more than ten times that of Haiti. Today, this nation of ten million has the largest economy in the Caribbean and the ninth largest in Latin America. I attribute this development to free and open trade policies that encourage foreign investment in factories—as well as to booming tourism, agriculture, and mining industries, and remittances from Dominicans in the United States.

The prosperity of the D.R. is a great example of the value of private sector participation in development, and of government policies that create good business conditions. If you look at the World Bank's development indicators for the D.R., you see a correlate rise in human well-being, including an increase in average life span and school enrollment and a decrease in poverty. The country has also experienced progress in the form of investment in environmental sustainability. As a visitor, you see development in obvious ways, such as smooth, paved roads all over the island, cell phones, high-tech stop lights, motor scooters, and cars. Santo Domingo has modern shopping malls and even a Bentley and Maserati dealer. Business investment is a good safeguard for the continuation of these developments.

The apparel industry has both contributed to and benefited from this growth. Since buying Timberland, VF has invested $23 million in health and safety initiatives and machine upgrades at the D.R. facility, and in social responsibility programs that impact the larger community. At the factory, you see safety measures such as sewing needle disposal boxes, first aid kits, and fire extinguishers. The workers, dressed in jeans and Timberland T-shirts of different colors, wear earplugs and safety glasses. (You have to don safety glasses and earplugs to tour the facility, too.) Some workers also wear gloves, finger protectors, and/or safety boots. Each machine has a little sign on it listing the safety equipment required to use it. There is a health clinic, as well as two full-time doctors on-site at Timberland, to help with everything from prenatal education to general health. Improving worker comfort can also involve a lot of little tweaks, such as adding a white lining to the high ceiling of a warehouse to reduce interior heat.

The spread of certification programs is one step toward improving factories worldwide, and Timberland D.R. operates in accordance with a handful of them, including the Worldwide Responsible Accredited Production program (WRAP). WRAP is based on workplace standards aligned with the International Labour Organization's conventions and it sets guidelines for hours, pay, benefits, and the health and safety of employees. WRAP certification prohibits child or forced labor, and requires compliance with local laws and international importing and exporting rules. A WRAP-certified factory also voluntarily commits to passing along these expectations to suppliers and contractors. Auditors come in for three- to four-day-long visits to check compliance.

The Timberland factory is also ISO 14000 certified, another audit-based program related to environmental management and reducing negative environmental impact. Finally, VF's own auditors can also drop in unannounced. All this oversight means that pretty much everyone at the factory is trying to live up to the highest standards every day. Maintaining all these certifications may sound like a lot of extra work, but certifications help businesses establish and maintain good protocols that benefit employees, the environment, and ultimately, the bottom line. As Schneider puts it, "They keep you on track."

Boots start with leather, which arrives at the factory pre-dyed from tanneries in the United States or Europe that meet the company's sustainability requirements. Skins of yellow, blue, black, and pink leather are stacked high in the sorting area, which resembles the self-service section of IKEA with its high ceilings hung with rows of fluorescent lights, its industrial-strength fans, and orange metal shelving units filled with bags and boxes of matching items. A big sign that reads "Sorting" in block letters hangs from the ceiling.

After the leather is sorted, it goes to the cutting room. Big, flat, metal cutting dies—each shaped like the front toe of a boot and labeled by shoe size—hang on the wall. You can hear the buzz of machines all around. Operators with yellow earplugs and purple T-shirts load the dies into the machines, lay the leather underneath, and then swing the press over the leather, pushing down to cut the shapes. They then stack together the cut pieces and send them on their way.

In the Stitching section (also identified by an overhead sign), operators sit on high stools with padded backs and metal footrests, facing pedal-operated sewing machines. The atmosphere is focused and calm. They wear earplugs and safety glasses as they carefully guide the leather. It's hard work (as I discovered at Wrangler and also while visiting a nearby Vans factory), but the setting is quite different from a sweatshop-style cut-and-sew facility. In a sweatshop, workers sit hunched over machines, crammed into an airless room, squinting in inadequate lighting. Here, there is plenty of air and light, and workers looks healthy, occupied, and dignified.

In another section, a different group of workers, wearing red smocks over T-shirts, apply white glue with paintbrushes to what will become the upper section of the boot. They then clip the glued uppers to a conveyor belt that hangs overhead and loops around, like a crazy freeway system, or like a chairlift for boots. The uppers ride to another section, where they are clipped to a rack to await insulation. Here, operators pair thick pieces of insulation with the leather, squeeze them together, and run the "sandwich" through yet another sewing machine. (There's no way I could get this material through one of those sewing machines!)

After insulation comes attaching the soles, a huge event in itself. It is unbelievable how much work goes into these boots! The classic waterproof yellow boot retails for just under $200 on the Timberland website. Even if you're not someone who ordinarily spends nearly $200 on a pair of shoes, when you see the work that goes into making a pair of boots, this price seems totally reasonable. It's definitely humbling to realize how much effort, material, and ingenuity goes into a pair of shoes we might easily buy for one season, then bury under other, newer purchases.

The room for making moccasins—the name Timberland gives its boat shoes—feels a little like a soccer match. It's all men in this section, and they're shouting to each other, arms flying through the air as they plunge two needles at a time through the leather. More than a hundred men are here, standing in long rows facing each other, each with a moccasin-in-progress on a metal form before him. The men shove the needles into the leather, pull the threads through the hole, spread their arms wide, and snap them tight. The moccasin workers are paid by the piece, a fact that adds to the energy and rush.

Like so many companies today, Timberland has a custom option, a way for customers to choose their own color combinations and logo applications. These boots are made in a separate section, and some of the combinations are really pretty. There's a navy and gray pair; a navy and white pair with a gold Timberland logo; black leather with red trim; and a very flashy red and tan pair.

In another building comes the end of the line, literally, for these boots: the testing room. This small, air-conditioned space feels like a science lab. Here, a selection of boots from each lot is tested. In one test, two pairs of boots are clamped at the toes, while a machine moves their heels up and down again and again to assess the durability of the sole. In another room, a pair of classic yellow boots, their tops covered by a plastic bag, are dipped up and down in a tub of water to test for leaks.

VF is in the process of replacing old buildings with new, air-conditioned ones (as opposed to using tons of fans) and upgrading old machines. In one of these new buildings, two operators pore over each piece of leather, marking imperfections. Then the leather is laid on a new, super-high-tech machine, and a laser beam cuts out the pieces around the marks. It calculates how to get the most pieces and the least amount of scrap (the way you might position cookie cutters on dough to cut the most cookies without having to reroll).

This machine will replace the hand-cutting. We worry about mechanization replacing human workers, as if "factory made" and "handmade" are on opposite ends of the spectrum, both from a process and from an ethical standpoint. But in this case, technology will mean less fabric waste, and the growing demand for Timberland products, at least for now, means cutters here can be retrained for another section. The United States was once the main buyer of Timberland boots, but now Asia and Europe account for 40 percent of the boots and shoes made here, and demand in these parts of the world shows little sign of letting up. In the emerging-economy nations of Brazil, China, India, Mexico, and Russia, apparel sales grew eight times faster in the past decade than they did in the United States, Canada, Germany, and the United Kingdom.

When it comes to mechanization, we can't blindly cling to the processes of the past any more than we can automatically assume all factories are demeaning or that every innovation is for the better. We have to assess and adjust and take into account the sustainability of changes.

A FACTORY AS A GOOD CITIZEN

It takes a lot of energy to run the sewing machines and the heavy sole-gluing equipment used in mass production of boots. Timberland plants trees in Santiago to mitigate its environmental footprint and works to reduce waste by recycling the cardboard and paper used at the factory and selling other waste products. Profits from these sales partially help fund additional social programs.

Timberland has a long tradition of community involvement in Santiago, which the acquisition by VF has expanded. Involving employees publicly helps them feel proud of the company and of themselves, starting a cycle of goodwill, says Schneider. "It's better for us if workers can see that we're helping the community and if we get all the employees involved in community service," he says. "We also try to help out in Haiti."

Pedro Jimenez, the manager of Projects, Sustainability, and Corporate Social Responsibility at Timberland D.R., has worked at this factory for more than two decades. He's excited about the increased focus on responsibility. "A big company can really transform how factories work in this nation. Everyone wants to do business with VF, so it's an amazing opportunity to share these practices. We have a big name and reputation, which helps us get others involved."

One such effort is the company's Global Stewards program. Through this program, employees volunteer for two-year terms to help drive Timberland's corporate social responsibility agenda at their specific location. A big wooden sign praising the Global Stewards hangs on the wall in the main office in the D.R. facility.

Involving employees in the broader social mission is part of creating a quality culture, says Jimenez, who talks excitedly about the CSR objectives and nonprofit partnerships. Jimenez highlights a handful of other programs that the company and its employees are involved in: painting and refurbishing a school for the deaf and teaching its students about environmental awareness; planting a garden and painting a local public elementary school attended by the kids of many workers; adding a water tower and filtration system at a school where bad water (not caused by the factory) was creating stomach problems for the kids; and building a plant nursery program at a new park in town, where employees help nurture 500,000 trees that will be donated to the community.

The new park is located directly across from a huge public high school, and kids cut through it after school on their way home, leaving behind the car fumes and honking horns of Santiago as they stroll on a stone walkway that winds through new-growth, indigenous trees forming a thick canopy overhead.

The company is also involved in all sorts of local projects with NGOs. One such group, Kites of Hope, has worked for a decade to stop impoverished children from working in landfills, where they would ferret out potentially valuable trash to sell. Kites of Hope helps these children get back into school. Jimenez talks proudly of one child from a desperately poor family who had been working in the landfill, finally returned to school through the help of Kites of Hope, went on to college, and is currently pursuing a master's degree at a university in Spain.

Timberland also has a long relationship with a day center for homeless kids in Santiago called Acción Callejera. Since 1989, Acción Callejera has been providing a safe place for kids to shower, eat, learn, and get social services. It's currently housed in a former private social club painted a cheery yellow, with ornate moldings, high ceilings, and a grand staircase. It's a quiet, airy, special-feeling place. Acción Callejera also offers skill development through games and creative projects, as well as therapy, medical and dental assistance, and reading and writing instruction to help kids catch up on what they've missed in school by being on the streets.

When kids come in, they can leave their tools in a front locker; many of the kids have shoe-shining kits or other supplies for scraping out a living. Acción Callejera also works with parents, when possible, to help curb family violence or provide food. Many of the forty or fifty homeless children and teens who use the center today are Haitians, youth who were trafficked or perhaps sent by their parents, or who paid to cross the border into the Dominican Republic in hopes of a better life. The center often tries to reconnect these kids, aged seven to seventeen, with their families back in Haiti. It also offers services to another four hundred or so at-risk kids in the local communities.

Over the years, Timberland has donated supplies, furniture, and shoes to the center. Timberland is currently involved in supporting a microenterprise here that will combine the company's own waste reduction goals with generating income for the center. A volunteer from the Japanese governmental aid agency Japan International Cooperation Agency (JICA) is designing key chains to be fashioned from leather—super-cute cats and other animals made from the many colors of boot scrap. The plan is for men in the local prison's leather craft program to teach volunteers and some employees how to work the leather. (Kids over the age of seventeen can legally work, as can the parents of kids in the community.) Acción Callejera hopes to sell the key chains on site and through retail partners such as the local grocery store, and to use these funds to help pay for their services.

I'm excited about this key-chain project; small- and medium-batch makers like this are important. I love them so much that I've built a business around them! But they don't provide every single thing we want or need, nor does small or artisanal necessarily mean ethical, as I've learned. My own personal style relies on the talents of so many people, both those working at factories for brands like Timberland or Gap, and those working in cottage industries.

Mass production is responsible for so many of the things we wear, use, and drive. I can't imagine living without jeans (which I clearly can't make). If I had to sew my own clothes, I'd be reduced to walking around in a blanket with a hole cut in the middle for my head. We need to move past black-and-white definitions of "good and bad actors" to buy the change we want to see—and to get dressed in the morning.

CHAPTER SIX

JUST DESSERTS FOR EVERYONE

Making Chocolate Sweet for the Farmers Who Grow It

He turned and reached behind him for the chocolate bar, then he turned back again and handed it to Charlie. Charlie grabbed it and quickly tore off the wrapper and took an enormous bite . . . The sheer blissful joy of being able to fill one's mouth with rich solid food!

—ROALD DAHL, FROM *CHARLIE AND THE CHOCOLATE FACTORY*

On a cold and rainy weekend in November, eighty of the world's best chocolate makers gathered together inside Seattle's Pier 91 cruise terminal, greeting colleagues, chatting with friends, and tasting chocolate. This lovefest for chocolate, also known as the annual Northwest Chocolate Festival, is the biggest and most important artisanal chocolate event in North America. It brings together independent chocolate makers, bakers, equipment manufacturers, and regular folk, all willing to pay thirty dollars a day to taste samples, meet the visionaries, and listen to lectures on everything from the origins of the beans to the art of making truffles from an ingredient that one visitor called "the world's most perfect food."

The two-story, tin-roofed terminal building was crowded and loud, the buzz due to the poor acoustics, the curtain "walls" delineating each chocolate display area, and the fact that attendees were basically eating nothing but chocolate all day. (Being at a chocolate festival can really make you crave a nice salad.) Despite the crowd, everyone was smiling, grinning ear to ear. How could they not? As anyone who loves chocolate can tell you, chocolate boosts endorphins, packs powerful antioxidants, and activates the same brain regions as those that fire when you're in love.

Most attendees seemed pretty serious about their sweets. They were taking notes, inquiring about the country of origin, snapping photos, or trying to decide if they should source from Guatemala or Ecuador when they start their own chocolate business.

This is a realistic question because it's easier than ever for individuals to make and sell fine chocolate. Only a handful of the companies displaying at the festival existed fifteen years ago; many started within the last five years. Even chocolate bar companies that are staples for many chocolate connoisseurs today, such as Scharffen Berger, Chocolove, or Taza, are relatively new entrants into the chocolate industry. In 2000, there were maybe five craft chocolate makers operating in the United States. Today, there are something like two hundred of these companies, from small to large, making chocolate from the bean and selling bars to the public. The entire craft chocolate industry is basically a bunch of start-ups. During the past decade or so, independent chocolate makers have sprung up in New York and California, Seattle and Florida, Minnesota, Utah, Wisconsin, and states in between. There are husband-and-wife chocolate-making teams, CEOs-turned-chocolate-activists, backpackers-turned-cacao-exporters, and a few swashbuckling, Indiana Jones types who travel the world for exotic cacao.

Chocolate is a competitive industry, but the atmosphere at the Northwest Chocolate Festival felt cooperative and supportive. Everyone recommended talking to someone else. "Go meet the people from Uncommon Cacao; they are really at the forefront of working to raise the standard of living for farmers!" said one craft maker. "You need to talk to Carlos, who sources from Colombia," said Emily Stone, cofounder of Uncommon Cacao. "Valrhona is an inspiration to me. They make a good product, source well, and pay a good price for their beans," said Greg D'Alesandre of the San Francisco–based Dandelion Chocolate and coauthor of *Making Chocolate: From Bean to Bar to S'More.*

TASTES GOOD, DOES GOOD

Chocolate starts on the tree as cacao in odd, Nerf football–shaped pods of red or yellow or orange growing straight from the trunk and hanging from the branches. Each pod contains about fifty cacao beans swaddled in gooey white fruit. These beans, after being scooped out, fermented, dried, and ground for hours or even days, get made into chocolate. Cacao was named by famous Swedish botanist Carl Linnaeus in the 1800s as Theobroma cacao, or "food-of-the-gods cacao," a good description for the popular treat made from the bean.

With regard to sourcing cacao ethically at the farm, the small craft chocolate makers are the real leaders. Almost all craft chocolate makers have a story to tell about their passion for working with chocolate—and improving the lives of those who grow it. They're sourcing directly from farmers or through cooperatives, helping increase yield and quality, and paying as much as three times the commodity price for raw beans. Some chocolate entrepreneurs got into it as a way to improve the lives of Central American farmers. Others seek to raise the standard of living for women and to transform local economies in chocolate-growing regions. Some were looking for a business that would let them work with a product that brings joy. One young maker in Hawaii decided he needed to do something more meaningful with his life than surf, and he hit upon starting a chocolate company using locally grown cacao.

Many chocolate makers are focused on the environment. Like Coffee, cacao is grown in the equatorial band on both sides of the equator, primarily by small-scale farmers, often in regions that are key areas of biodiversity—spots that provide habitats for birds, lizards, and other trees. Also like coffee, cacao can be grown under the shade of larger trees, making it an environmentally friendly crop, if grown in that way. Shade-grown cacao production is one way environmentalists are looking to preserve and bring back biodiversity and reduce deforestation. Cacao plants are also similar to coffee in that they're vulnerable to climate change, and there is a great deal of concern in the chocolate industry about the long-term viability of the crop, not just among craft makers, but also by the major brands. Many leading environmental nonprofits and research institutions are also focused on creating a sustainable cacao sector.

The craft chocolate movement is also about taste. Mass-market chocolate, sometimes called industrial chocolate, can certainly be fun to eat and provide an instant pick-me-up, but the focus of these companies has long been low cost and consistent flavor, leading to bars and chips made from blends of lower-grade cacao mixed with a significant amount of sugar and often artificial ingredients such as vanillin and the emulsifier soy lecithin. Craft chocolate makers, on the other hand, look to winemakers, craft beer creators, and farm-to-table chefs for inspiration. As with these other movements, today's chocolate entrepreneurs are after high quality and high impact, and finding unique flavor profiles from specific regions and beans. Many of the craft makers are devoted to the bean-to-bar movement—controlling all aspects of the final product, from how the cacao is grown at the farm to how the label looks in the store. They are artisans on a quest to expand the possibilities of taste.

I love chocolate because, well . . . the taste. And texture. I love all types of chocolate. I like getting a Hershey's bar, or a chocolate chip cookie, or a jar of a great chocolate dessert sauce made with heavy cream by a Houston-based company I recently discovered called Somebody's Mother's.

Chocolate plays an important role in society, too. It's a delicious treat and also a social lubricant, something we give to show affection, increase trust, or boost morale. Chocolate often serves as a gift, a way to say that we care. It's an offering of friendship or romance or consolation that's immediately understood.

In my own life, chocolate played an important role in my budding entrepreneurship. As a little girl, I had the total joy of being a Daisy and then a Brownie in the Girl Scouts program. Like other Girl Scouts, I sold cookies. My favorite Girl Scout cookies are the top sellers, Thin Mints and Caramel deLites (also called Samoas)—both covered in chocolate. When I was in first grade, the Girl Scouts had an incentive program to motivate girls to push more cookies; cookie sales actually generate significant revenue for the nonprofit. There was a catalog of things top sellers could earn, including a pink Barbie Corvette and a real bicycle.

To me, a bicycle was the biggest thing a person could get. It was the best present you might receive for Christmas, the one your parents would hide in the back and bring out at the very end. I had a bike, but the idea that I could have *two*, that a seven-year-old had the opportunity to earn something like that, was mind-boggling. It was like winning a car today. It made me recognize the value of being incentivized to reach a goal, especially in sales, and the motivating power of personal reward.

The experience with Girl Scout cookies also taught me how important healthy competition is. I remember very clearly the positive energy in the troop, the desire to see which girls could sell the most. It wasn't a negative; it was a motivation. We were all encouraging one another rather than hoping others would fail. The more each girl sold, the better your whole troop would do.

I'm a natural saleswoman, I discovered (with somewhat mixed feelings). I wanted to be strategic about it, even back then. I asked my mother to give me the phone numbers of all the families who lived on one of the nicest streets in town, River Oaks Boulevard, a wide lane of stately homes leading to the country club. I thought, *Surely these people can buy a lot of cookies!* My mom did not want me to call up people I didn't know and try to sell them cookies over the phone. (Nor was it clear that she actually had the phone number of every single resident on the street.) She countered by offering to drive me there and let me go door to door. For better or worse, I'd already focused on the role of purchasing power to make a difference.

Despite my positive memories of chocolate, and the near-universal affection for it, this sweetest of all foods has a very sour history from a labor and environmental perspective, when it comes to industrial chocolate sourcing. While craft chocolate makers are forming fair working relationships with smallholder farmers in Central and South America and the Caribbean, two-thirds of the world's cacao supply still comes from the West African countries of Ghana and Côte d'Ivoire. Cacao farming in these regions is notoriously rife with labor exploitation, from slavery to child labor to human trafficking. The average cacao farmer in Ghana makes eighty-four cents a day, while farmers in Côte d'Ivoire earn about fifty cents a day. Countries supplying cacao rely upon it economically and can be less than eager to expose labor exploitation that might drive buyers away. Cacao farming is also a cause of massive deforestation, destruction of animal habitat, and decimation of animals in West Africa—even within supposedly protected forests.

The Nestlé company, which buys 414,000 tons of cacao a year, says that the challenges with cleaning up the supply chain are complicated because so many cacao farmers are poor and have small plots of land with low productivity due to depleted soil and old trees that haven't been replaced with newer, higher-yielding ones. As Nestlé's official literature puts it, "They often resort to using their children for tasks that could be harmful to their physical or mental development and are therefore classified as child labor. Women in the cocoa supply chain are often under-rewarded for their work, or not given a voice in their communities."

Andrew Savitz writes about cacao farming in his classic book on sustainable business, *The Triple Bottom Line*. As he explains, children in these countries can be "pulled from school, forced to work in the cacao fields and factories, and frequently injured on the job. Human rights activists have been protesting these conditions for years, and a number of food companies have responded with substantive changes."

Chocolate is part of the livelihood of some estimated fifty million people worldwide, more than five million of whom are smallholder cocoa farmers. The United States is a huge buyer of chocolate, and the industry here provides nearly seventy thousand jobs in chocolate and candy manufacturing alone.

Before the explosion of craft chocolate makers, there was very little pressure from competitors on chocolate companies to clean up the supply chain. A few major retail players and large-scale traders dominated the chocolate industry. You could buy bars at the grocery store from Hershey's, Nestlé, Mars, or even Cadbury. You might get a box of chocolates from Whitman's or Fanny Farmer at the drugstore, or find high-end bonbons at a European chocolate boutique, or from a local confectioner using chocolate purchased from an established chocolate manufacturer to make and sell candy.

Then in 1997, Scharffen Berger began operating in San Francisco. This was the first independent chocolate maker of any real size in the United States in more than fifty years. The company sought out high-quality cacao from, among other places, Madagascar. They turned out chocolate bars that were dark and deep, complex and smoldering—similar to something you might buy from an established French chocolate maker like Valrhona. But these were made in America by a former lawyer and a former doctor. The bars were sophisticated and delicious, taking their cue, in part, from the wine and local food culture of the Bay Area.

Scharffen Berger was an instant hit among serious chocolate lovers. The Hershey Company took note, and in 2005 bought the craft chocolate maker for a reported $50 million. The next year, Hershey bought Dagoba, an organic, Rainforest Alliance Certified company founded in 2001 in Oregon by Frederick Schilling. Suddenly, other chocolate lovers realized that a market existed for high-end chocolate bars. These sales to Hershey ignited a wave of would-be chocolate makers and hobbyists to set up shop and go professional. As food writer Megan Giller says in her book, *Bean-to-Bar Chocolate: America's Craft Chocolate Revolution*, chocolate lovers recognized a real economic possibility. "They saw the event as the turning point in their careers, when they knew that their passion had to shift from a hobby into a business," Giller writes.

Technology also plays a part in today's craft chocolate entrepreneurship. Improved communication, easier access to cacao growers, and an ever-growing online marketplace help facilitate start-ups. Online education also aids would-be chocolate creators. Many leading small-scale chocolate makers watched videos about making chocolate at home on the website Chocolate Alchemy, run by the now-legendary (in the chocolate world) John Nanci, who has been called "the godfather of kitchen-counter chocolatiering" by the *New York Times*. Some chocolate makers watched YouTube videos showing how to build roasters, grinders, and shellers from ordinary appliances like hair dryers, Shop-Vacs, and meat grinders.

For others, the introduction of small, inexpensive professional chocolate-making machines lowered the barrier to entry. When Scharffen Berger started, they were working in a huge, industrial-sized space filled with professional chocolate-making equipment from Europe—big, heavy, metal grinders and mixers, the kinds of machines that look like works of art themselves and cost tens of thousands of dollars. But chocolate can be made in smaller batches with lighter, less costly equipment, as a husband-and-wife team in Atlanta realized.

Andal Balu and Dr. Balu Balasubramanian, two scientists originally from India, launched CocoaTown in 2007. Before CocoaTown, they were running a company from their home base in Georgia that sold kitchen appliances for authentic Indian cooking. CocoaTown sells stainless steel grinders that can fit into an ordinary kitchen, as well as all the other pieces of equipment needed to turn cacao into chocolate—the roaster, cracker, cooling tray, winnower, and melangeur.

These little machines can make anywhere from one to one hundred pounds of chocolate, and you can buy an entire set of their entry-level line for about $5,000. Many small craft makers working today started on CocoaTown machines and still use them. There still isn't a Starbucks in the world of chocolate—no one major player raising the price per pound and habituating consumers to paying more for better-sourced, higher-quality beans. But taken as a whole, today's small-batch makers are offering substantial, ethically sourced options for chocolate consumers. You can find out a great deal about the bars on the shelf. "Look for chocolate from a company that gives real information about the region the cacao is from, the farmers, and why this or that program they support matters. If it's not on the bar, check their website," says Maricel Presilla, chef, food historian, cacao importer, and author of *The New Taste of Chocolate.*

The big companies are starting to notice—as the sales of Scharffen Berger and Dagoba to Hershey indicate. Some people in the craft industry are optimistic about their collective influence. "We know we're putting some pressure on the cacao industry because they talk to us," says Greg D'Alesandre of Dandelion. "They ask us what we're doing, and how."

Craft chocolate makers are also influencing the larger industry by helping develop new sources of cacao. Many are looking closer to home at regions with good cacao genetics (or varieties) and no long history of labor exploitation in cacao. Craft makers are working with smallholder farmers, farmer cooperatives, and companies in Ecuador, Colombia, Guatemala, Peru, and the Caribbean. They're helping improve the crop at the source and sharing information with consumers about who exactly is growing these beans. They are showing the rest of the chocolate-producing (and chocolate-eating) world that chocolate companies can thrive while paying more than the commodity price for quality cacao that is grown in ethical and sustainable ways.

Meanwhile, various nonprofits like Mighty Earth and leaders in other countries, such as Prince Charles with his International Sustainability Unit, are exposing chocolate's dark side to consumers and helping push the major manufacturers and traders to address labor exploitation and environmental destruction.

FROM BEAN TO BAR IN THE DOMINICAN REPUBLIC

You hear the pounding beat of merengue music everywhere in the Dominican Republic—at hotels, in squares, at weddings and parties—along with bachata, salsa, and reggaeton. Is all this music and dancing due to chocolate? Seems possible. The D.R., it turns out, is not only home to good factories like Timberland but is also the world leader in certified organic cacao. Cacao was first cultivated in South and Central America. The tree was brought to the D.R. by the Spanish in the 1600s and further developed by the French. Today, you'll find old varieties and new hybrids of cacao growing in the dense, tangled cloud forests in the northern part of the island and in rolling green hills to the east.

In the craft chocolate world, the D.R. is known as the go-to source for nearly every company getting started because of its organic cacao and its proximity to the United States. There are direct flights to the D.R.'s three airports from many cities on the Eastern Seaboard. This, along with good roads and cell phone service, makes it easy for would-be (and established) chocolate makers to visit farms and do business.

HOW TO TALK CHOCOLATE

Cacao vs. Cocoa: These terms are used somewhat interchangeably. *Cacao* generally refers to the plant—a small, tropical evergreen tree whose flowers turn into gourd-like pods that each hold about fifty seeds within. These seeds are called "cacao beans" (or, to confuse matters, sometimes "cocoa beans") and are the beginning of chocolate. *Cocoa* is the powdered form of chocolate used for hot and cold chocolate milk, and it is one product that can be made from cacao. There are two kinds of cocoa powder. Dutched cocoa (what's inside a packet of hot chocolate mix) has been treated with an alkaline solution to make it easier to mix with liquid. Natural cocoa powder has not been alkalized. (Some companies will label their non-alkalized cocoa powder *cacao* to differentiate it from Dutched cocoa and perhaps to make it sound more authentic.)

Cocoa Nibs: Cocoa nibs have become an increasingly popular consumer item, and I love the company Sweetriot, which sells them in a tin. Cocoa nibs are crunchy, chewy little pieces of broken cocoa bean, about the size of a sunflower seed, that you can eat out of your hand. Cocoa nibs are made after the cacao pod has been picked, the beans scooped out, and then fermented, dried, roasted, and winnowed (had the thin shell or seed skin removed).

Chocolate Liquor vs. Chocolate Liqueur: If cocoa nibs aren't packaged to be eaten (and they usually aren't), they get ground into chocolate liquor, which isn't alcoholic at all but rather a thick, unsweetened mass of chocolate, sometimes called "chocolate mass." Chocolate liquor can then be made into eating chocolate, or separated into cocoa butter and a cocoa cake that can be ground and sifted into cocoa powder. *Chocolate liqueur* is an alcoholic drink, usually made from a vodka base and chocolate flavoring. (Some people have tried making a liqueur out of the husks of cocoa beans, but not with any widespread commercial success.)

Cocoa Butter vs. Butter: Cocoa beans are naturally 54 percent fat by weight, and all this fat is *cocoa butter,* which is derived by pressing chocolate liquor into its constituent parts of cocoa butter and the dry cocoa cake. (If you eat a cocoa bean, the cocoa butter makes it taste fatty and waxy, unlike a coffee bean, which is far harder and drier.) Cocoa butter is 100 percent nondairy. *Butter* is a dairy product, unrelated to chocolate.

Chocolate Manufacturer vs. Chocolate Maker: A *chocolate manufacturer* is a large company that makes any number of chocolate products from cocoa beans for the mass market, with perhaps a specialty line. Think Hershey's. A *chocolate maker* also turns cacao into chocolate, but perhaps has a personal relationship with the cacao farmer, a focus on fine flavor, and a smaller, more specialized market of chocolate connoisseurs. Many chocolate makers today consider themselves *chocolate artisans* or *craft chocolatiers.* Think Dandelion, Dick Taylor Craft Chocolate, or most of the bars you find at a Whole Foods, a gourmet market, or in the specialty section of your grocery store.

Chocolate vs. Candy: Serious chocolate makers differentiate between what they do—turn cacao into a great-tasting food—and what candy makers do, which is buy chocolate in bulk from someone else to make fun sweets that may or may not have high-quality chocolate involved, or even all that much chocolate. As Dan Bieser from the Wisconsin-based craft chocolate company Tabal put it, "We don't make candy. We make food. And it's called chocolate."

Couverture: The name given for bulk chocolate made by a chocolate manufacturer or chocolate maker and bought by candy makers, bakers, and restaurant chefs for making candy and dessert. Couverture can be very high quality. It generally has more cocoa butter added to the chocolate than is typical in a chocolate candy bar, enabling it to melt more easily and flow more smoothly over a truffle, say, or a cake pop. Your menu might read, "Chocolate-covered cheesecake," but the chef ordered couverture to make that dessert.

Milk Chocolate vs. Dark Chocolate: *Milk chocolate* has milk added to it, in the form of milk solids and fat. It also usually has a lower percentage of cacao than dark chocolate. The popular Hershey's milk chocolate bar (perfect for making s'mores) has 11 percent cacao. The FDA requires a bar to have 10 percent cacao in it to be labeled "chocolate." *Dark chocolate* has no milk at all and may contain anywhere from 55 to 85 percent cacao, an amount usually noted on the wrapper. (Dark chocolate lovers so often look down on milk chocolate as a lesser version that a *New York Times* article about the new "dark milk" chocolate bars attempted to challenge this bias. The article cited "suave" bars by San Francisco–based Guittard, Seattle-based Theo, Scharffen Berger, Michel Cluizel, and Valrhona as particularly good options.) "Don't be intimidated by chocolate artisans who say, 'It has to be 90 percent cacao for me,'" insists Julian Rose, a chef and master chocolatier of Moonstruck Chocolate in Portland, Oregon. "Most people like milk chocolate, even if they eat it in the closet, in the dark."

Terroir: This French word, long used to help describe wine, means "territory"—as in the place where a grape (or cacao pod) grows. A location's soil composition, sun, rain, mulch, frost, etc. affect the flavor of the produce grown there. As chocolate makers pursue and attempt to convey greater understanding of cacao flavor, they increasingly discuss terroir.

White Chocolate: This is candy. There's no actual cacao in it, just a huge amount of cocoa butter and sugar, along with milk solids and milk fat, lecithin, and vanilla (and maybe little googly eyes and a sugar nose, if it's an Easter bunny).

The D.R. is also known in the chocolate world for its high-quality cacao "genetics"—the term cacao professionals use to describe the type of cacao plant—which makes the not-too-difficult trip doubly worth it. The taste of a chocolate bar is affected by how the crop is grown, the postharvest technique, the skill of the chocolate maker, and the specific type of cacao plant.

Another major draw of the D.R. is its well-developed, sophisticated cacao infrastructure. In the vast majority of the cacao-growing world, smallholder farmers grow the beans, ferment and dry them, and then sell them to whoever is buying—usually middlemen or coyotes. This decentralized, every-farmer-for-himself approach leaves growers vulnerable to accepting whatever price they can get from whatever buyer wanders past. If no one comes by to buy the beans, the farmer's haul that day might rot, meaning no income from that load. It also means inconsistent flavor from farm to farm because the beans are fermented and dried in different, and often haphazard ways.

In the D.R., in contrast, a handful of producers buy wet beans from farmers—as in, scooped out of the cacao pods and dumped in a bucket or sack. The producers then handle the fermenting and drying and selling, adding value to the crop by constantly working to improve their processes. This centralized system makes the quality of the cacao consistent. The high-quality beans also bring higher prices, and the producers have far more bargaining power than an individual farmer does. As D'Alesandre of Dandelion Chocolate puts it, "In the D.R., a big producer like the family-owned Rizek can say to a craft maker, 'I can make exactly what you want, but you're going to pay for it.' Or the cooperative producer Conacado can say, 'We're a fair trade, certified organic co-op, and if you want our better beans, you will pay more for it.' It's also easier for the farmers. They can harvest the pods and get paid the next day, and they get a pretty good price."

The production facilities in the D.R. classify the beans as unfermented or fermented. Fermenting improves the flavor of the cacao and the resulting chocolate. Unfermented beans, usually the lower-quality ones (labeled "Sanchez" in the D.R.) are generally sold to big chocolate manufacturers to use in lower-end, candy-grade chocolate. The fermented beans, classified as "Hispaniola," are more expensive to buy and offer a richer, more complex taste. This classification system is another reason for the D.R.'s popularity as a cacao-producing region. Craft chocolate makers buy fermented beans exclusively, and in the D.R., they know what they're getting. Half of the sixty thousand tons of cacao produced annually in the D.R. is classified as Hispaniola, meaning half of what farmers produce earns them the higher price of the better product.

The D.R. is a role model for other cacao-growing countries. It's also a great example of the connection between private sector investment and economic and social development. Investment in the country by various types of businesses—in things like roads and telecommunications—has increased the ease of operation for many sectors, including cacao. People you meet working throughout the cacao sector, from small farmers to large producers, have completed high school and gone on to college. Unlike Haiti, where plastic bottles are everywhere, the highways and back roads in the D.R. are free of that kind of litter. The sidewalks in the well-preserved, historic Colonial Zone of the capital, Santo Domingo, are practically spotless. Most people have access to running water here, meaning there's less need for bottled water, and the development of recycling facilities also plays a part in the city's clean streets. In the D.R., it's easy to trace the positive social and environmental impact of a company paying more for high-quality cacao that ends up in higher-priced chocolate bars that you or I can decide to buy.

CACAO TOWN

The center of the cacao industry in the Dominican Republic is in San Francisco de Macorís, a city in the northern part of the island, north of Santo Domingo and west of Punta Cana, the oceanfront resort town on the island's eastern tip. While Punta Cana has become famous as a sun-and-sand destination, great for rest and relaxation, restaurants and nightclubs, golfing, all-inclusive family resorts, and sports like zip-lining, windsurfing, kayaking, and sailing, San Francisco de Macorís is a low-key agricultural center. It feels like a farming community in the United States, maybe like California's Central Valley—but a steamy, tropical version of it. There's a busy, utilitarian feeling to the place, with the focus on work and earning.

Chocolate makers, investors, and people working for nonprofits fly in and out of the airport in nearby Santiago. Everyone seems to know everyone else. A leader of the island's largest cacao producer, the cooperative Conacado, dropped by one of the town's two business hotels to share information with me about the group's social service programs. In the hotel restaurant, he paused to greet two young men from France who were in town to work on a development initiative funded by several French chocolate makers and led by Valrhona. At the ice cream store on the town's central square, the editor of the local paper greeted the founder of the island's smallest cacao exporter, Zorzal Cacao.

Most of the action in town happens at processing facilities and large office complexes. On the smooth, well-paved main road, you pass tin-roofed fermenting sheds and tentlike drying facilities. A huge white office building owned by Rizek, one of the largest cacao producers in the country, rises next to a Nestlé facility on the way to the headquarters of Öko-Caribe, a boutique-like producer that buys from 165 farmers working more than 1,000 hectares of organic land and sells to craft makers around the world.

The cacao itself grows in the hills to the north and to the east. Visiting a cacao farm in the wet and misty cloud forest up north can mean stepping into a pair of knee-high black rubber boots and then hiking through the jumbled-looking tropical farmland. You step on fallen leaves slick with rain, lower yourself gingerly down mud steps cut into the slope of a valley, hop across stones in a swirling creek, then climb back up a hill on the other side. You might see a macadamia tree with its huge canopy, and a tiny, speckled green lizard darting across a guava tree. Sweet lemons grow around you, and you can pick one off a tree to eat.

Cacao trees, tall and thin with oval leaves, are less distinctive looking than coffee trees. But the cacao pods themselves look like Christmas tree decorations from some far-off planet. They hang like colorful ornaments from the branches, sprouting off the sides of the trunks, and crowd together in clusters of orange, red, and yellow.

When you pull a ripe pod from the tree, it feels hard and slightly bumpy. You crack it open with a machete or by bashing it against the trunk. The cacao seeds are clumped together inside in one long, fat column covered with slick, white goo, clinging to the side of the pod like a small alien baby. You can pull off an individual bean and suck on it, the white, gooey fruit as sugary and tart as a SweeTart. The cacao beans themselves are bitter and waxy, the cocoa fat evident even in the raw state.

To begin the process of transforming these wet, pulp-covered beans into high-quality chocolate, farmers have only about six hours to get them from the cracked-open pods to the fermenting shed; any longer than that and the sugar of the fruit begins to turn bad, or even rot.

At Finca Elvesia, a historic cacao plantation in the island's eastern Hato Mayor region, beans are brought by horse from the highlands down to the finca's fermenting and drying sheds. The finca both grows and buys beans, and handles the drying and fermenting. Finca Elvesia was founded in the late 1800s by Swiss immigrants, and its rolling green hills, big sky, and little manager's house resemble Switzerland (minus the snowcapped mountains, plus palm trees).

Fermenting sheds look more or less the same everywhere on the island. Generally, you see three levels of big wooden fermenting boxes with oxidized metal hinges. They look like giant steamer trunks, or maybe old treasure chests. The wet beans are dumped into the top row of fermenting boxes, then covered with banana leaves. They sit there for about two days, then are moved down to a second box for a couple more days, and then a third. The fermenting happens naturally, as yeast from the cacao pods (and the machetes, insects, and workers' hands) "eats" the sugary white goo enveloping the beans. Fresh air and bacteria mix with the beans during each move, helping with the fermentation.

You can feel the heat from fermentation if you hold your hand over an open box. If you move aside the banana leaves and reach down into the beans, you feel a slimy, slippery mess that eventually reaches 120 degrees, much hotter than a hot tub. When you pull your hand out, the now-brown goo sticks to your fingers.

After fermenting, the beans are transported to long, low drying tents with domed tops, and spread out on wire mesh drying tables or, as at Finca Elvesia, on elevated wooden platforms. They're still in their skins at this stage and look like whole almonds. In the D.R., many drying sheds have indoor blowers or heat lamps to combat the humidity of the island. Cacao beans have to reach a specific level of dryness before they can be packed in huge sacks to ship.

Like many producers here, Finca Elvesia cultivates both fermented and unfermented beans, selling them at different prices to different markets. You can taste the difference raw. At Finca Elvesia, it's so hot in the drying tent that the beans are warm and crisp and have a roasty flavor. The fermented bean has a more complex, slightly wine-like taste, even in its raw state.

Finca Elvesia sells Rainforest Alliance Certified and certified organic cacao to many craft makers, including Dick Taylor Chocolate, Taza, and Scharffen Berger. After Hershey aquired Scharffen Berger, the company continued to source from Finca Elvesia and to pay the premium for the certified, high-quality Hispaniola beans. This is a small part of Hershey's overall operations, but it's encouraging to see a major chocolate manufacturer being a good customer for a tiny farm like this.

Finca Elvesia employs about fifteen people full-time and another twenty or so temporary workers during the two annual harvests, many of them Haitians who have crossed over to the D.R. in search of work. There is on-site housing for some of the temporary workers, while others live down in one of the nearby villages.

Finca Elvesia currently exports its fermented and dried beans through Rizek, which also owns a variety of other businesses on the island. When Hurricane Georges hit the island in 1998, it damaged nearly all the cacao plantations. Rizek stepped in, helping farmers rehabilitate their lands with new trees and offering free training and education to help ensure the success of the newly planted trees. The company formed a social services foundation, called Fuparoca, to meet these needs in an ongoing way. "It's a two-way relationship," says José Efraín Camilo, Fuparoca's manager of compliance and certifications. "Fuparoca is a social hand of Rizek, designed to help the farmer. But better quality and higher yield also ensure the cacao bean we trade."

In 2004, Fuparoca began helping farmers obtain organic and other certifications, and it now employs about twenty agricultural technicians, or "agronomists," who have been educated at universities in San Francisco de Macorís, Santiago, or Santo Domingo. These agronomists travel to farms and production facilities all over the country, offering training and workshops in farming techniques and organic and sustainable cocoa plantation management.

Fuparoca has also improved the access roads and bridges leading to rural communities, which helps children get to school and family members get to work. The foundation works to identify water sources near communities that lack running water, and builds pumps and reservoirs to bring water to these families. The foundation also provides first aid kits and training, buys school supplies for about thirty rural elementary schools, and provides things like chairs, keyboards, chalkboards, and building upgrades. To me, this is another example of the kind of broadly beneficial, incentivized investment so evident in the D.R.

HARNESSING THE MARKET IS FOR THE BIRDS

About an hour north of San Francisco de Macorís, high up a winding, dirt road that turns to mud in the rain, is an organic cacao farm that is part of the nation's first private nature reserve. Called Reserva Zorzal, this 1,000-acre reserve and farm was created by an American named Charles Kerchner, along with the Moreno family of the D.R., and the New York–based Eddy Foundation. Kerchner is a glasses-wearing academic type who spends half his time swashbuckling around the lush, tropical cloud forest of this reserve-cum-cacao-farm, and the other half working as a land management consultant in the United States.

On the long drive up to Zorzal, you pass thick, new-growth trees blanketing the hills. These hills were recently used for cattle grazing and nearly deforested, but plants grow fast in the cloud forest. You finally arrive at a wide, grassy plateau, park in the short grass, step out of the truck (now caked with mud), and instantly smell chocolate—a very unexpected (and very welcome) scent to find wafting toward you high in the cloud forest.

The aroma comes from the beans fermenting in a warehouse and drying in the long, low sheds visible to the right, and from the melangeur—a chocolate mixer churning on a picnic table in the open-air ground floor of the farm's two-story office and welcome center. It's incredibly peaceful up here, the only sounds coming from a few birds chirping in the distance and the melangeur's metal wheels pushing liquid chocolate over and under and over again. The melangeur is about the size of a personal chocolate fountain you might buy at Target, but the chocolate here is actually being ground and mixed with sugar, not just cascaded.

To create a quality chocolate bar, the melangeur would have to continue grinding the sugar and chocolate particles down to five microns, the size necessary to be indiscernible by the tongue. This can take a full day in a tabletop model; large, professional chocolate makers use far bigger, more powerful machines. Some chocolate makers then dump this velvety, delicious liquid into yet another machine, called a *conche*, for more mixing. This molten chocolate is then tempered, a chemical process of heating and cooling that gives chocolate its nice sheen and satisfying snap when breaking. Tempered chocolate is poured into a mold to harden, then sold.

The rest of Zorzal's chocolate-making equipment sits in the tiny kitchen, basically a toaster-oven-size roaster and a grinder that looks like a home meat grinder. Zorzal Cacao is not a chocolate maker but rather a cacao farm and processor. The low-tech equipment here is to make samples for potential buyers, conservationists, students (and authors).

Dipping a spoon into liquid chocolate made from freshly picked and roasted beans is a high point of this farm tour. This isn't just bean to bar; it's tree to tongue, a truly amazing chance to be one with nature and with the all-natural "food of the gods."

Then it starts raining, that tropical-style downpour that begins in an instant, seemingly out of nowhere. It's so humid in the open-walled seating area already that the actual rain doesn't feel like a huge change. Why get up? (Especially when you're sipping espresso and licking molten chocolate from a spoon.)

Kerchner says he first visited the D.R. nearly twenty years ago while in the Peace Corps. Years later, while pursuing a PhD in forestry in Vermont, he was drawn to the D.R. again after learning that it is the winter home of a palm-size northeastern songbird called the Bicknell's thrush. Bird-watching is a big part of Vermont's summer tourism industry, but the female Bicknell thrush was disappearing from the Vermont woods. What was the cause? A diminishing food supply in the D.R. due to clear-cutting of the cloud forest. The question for Kerchner was not *if* conservation matters, but rather how to pay residents to not clear-cut their land and instead leave a habitat for the birds that split their time between the two nations.

He began looking for a business solution to the problem of land conservation and hit upon the idea of establishing a private reserve that would be funded, in part, by sales from an adjoining cacao farm. Working with the D.R.-based nonprofit Fundación Loma Quita Espuela and the Dominican Environmental Consortium, Kerchner created the Reserva Zorzal and Zorzal Cacao.

Today, a full two-thirds of Reserva Zorzal's land is the nature preserve, and Kerchner works to protect this critical area of biodiversity with a strategy similar to that of Conservation International and Starbucks with coffee—using sales from the cacao to pay for reserve management and hiring and helping locals to ensure its sustainability. Cacao plantations are very important to the biodiversity of the D.R. because they provide habitats for birds, reptiles, and butterflies, and rely on the continued growth of native trees for shade. The D.R. has more than six hundred rare plant species, as well as dozens of species of birds and reptiles, which makes it a biodiversity hotspot.

Kerchner also works with an international carbon standard called Plan Vivo to sell carbon offsets from the farm and from neighboring farms. Plan Vivo has established a protocol for carbon offsets in the voluntary market. Big companies (including JetBlue, Disney, and Google) "buy" carbon offsets around the world as part of their corporate social responsibility initiatives, essentially paying someone else to plant trees, or not cut down trees, to meet their own carbon reduction aims. Zorzal sells offsets to chocolate companies that buy cacao beans. If a company buys cacao from Zorzal, part of the cost per ton goes toward planting trees. Since starting, Zorzal has planted about 250 acres of trees through Plan Vivo, and farmers living in the buffer zone around the protected area are paid every year to maintain a healthy forest.

Reserva Zorzal also creates jobs in wildlife monitoring and boosts the income of nearby farmers by educating them on best practices and by buying their wet cacao. One-third of its own land is dedicated to growing super-high-quality cacao. The company then ferments and dries it with an artist-like quest for perfection, and sells it for around double the commodity price to equally passionate chocolate makers.

In the final stage of drying at Zorzal, the beans are moved to the last shed in the line, this one with a concrete floor. Everyone tiptoes around in socks, keeping the floor clean, while two workers shovel the beans around, turning them to complete the drying. One worker, wearing a green T-shirt that says *Hawaii*, sits at a table in the middle of the room, patiently cutting one hundred beans in half lengthwise and laying out the split-open pairs in rows before him. Kerchner or another worker grades the beans by looking at the cracks in them; the more cracks, the better the fermentation. If a batch is less than 80 percent fermented, the whole lot becomes grade B, which may be used for cocoa powder, nibs, and chocolate bar blends. The care these producers take with their beans is amazing. It's as if the special feeling of receiving a box of fine chocolates starts at the farm.

Marcos Antonio Lajara, or "Veho," grew up in the cloud forest near Zorzal and has been working in cacao most of his life. For years he sold beans to large producers, having to pay someone with a truck to bring them down the hill—a time-consuming, arduous journey that could lead to rotting beans. When Zorzal opened high in the hills, Veho began selling the beans he harvests to the company, and also working for it. The new cacao facility has made a huge difference in his life and the lives of other locals. "Before, this big farm had cows, and they would come into people's land or wander on the road. There was no employment for the people here," says Lajara.

The higher price for beans has enabled Lajara to continue improving the farm he manages (which is owned by a doctor in San Francisco de Macorís), and his home life. Despite the huge advances in the D.R. during the past couple of decades, rural communities like his still lack electricity and running water. Since working for Zorzal, he's been able to buy solar panels to generate energy at home. He and his wife and three children now have lights—and the Internet. (They still collect rainfall for drinking water.) The extra earnings have led to more food security, books, and clothes. Lajara also bought one of the little motorbikes you see everywhere in the D.R., which enables his children to get to school more easily. His oldest daughter, now twenty-one, has begun working at the Zorzal basecamp, cooking traditional Dominican dishes for visitors and coordinating visits.

Zorzal also built the road, such as it is. The difference this road has made to the community is huge, says Lajara. "It's like the difference between the dirt and the sky. The road and electricity are the most important things for rural people."

Lajara, slim and fit, is dressed in jeans, a T-shirt with the Puma logo, a baseball cap, and the black rubber boots you need to tromp around this area's muddy farmland. He looks at home in the Zorzal basecamp as he pulls up a chair and sits down. The small size of this operation has allowed Kerchner to get personally involved with the farmers he buys from. Recognizing the pride Lajara takes in the land, Kerchner encouraged him to start working as a nature and birdwatching guide for visitors. Kerchner also paid, with help from a grant, for Lajara to travel with him to the United States to learn more about conservation efforts and to meet the chocolate makers who ultimately use the beans.

Involving workers in the mission is part of the Zorzal vision. "We need the people we work with to understand what we're doing so they can make their own decisions about what's valuable," says Kerchner. "If you have the opportunity to go to Boston and Vermont and meet chocolate makers who use your beans, you get it. It's a development model, a way to 'show, not tell.' If he understands why it's important to produce the best cacao, it's better for us."

One of the chocolate makers that buys from Zorzal is Raaka chocolate in Brooklyn. In late 2017, Raaka signed a partnership deal with JetBlue Airways to provide chocolate—made from 100 percent Zorzal cacao—for little squares to be given to passengers flying in the airline's premium class cabin. I love this partnership because it means a big order from Zorzal that will raise the company's visibility and potentially help generate more clients. (Also, I think it's great for an airline to offer chocolate. I almost always travel with chocolate in my purse, and I love the idea of being able to replenish my supply on a plane.)

On the way back down to the city from Zorzal, the road is even muddier than in the morning, the afternoon's rain having pounded new gullies. Two small rivers have swollen over their bridges, and the truck has to forge through the water to keep going. A man leading two donkeys walks slowly downhill, each donkey carrying two huge sacks of yams on its back. The donkeys' fur is slick from the rain, and the saddle on one slips, spilling yams into the mud. The man halts his animals and begins the slow process of retrieving the yams. Economic development can feel like this—two steps forward, one step back—a nation with a Bentley and a Maserati dealer in the capital city, and rural farmers transporting produce on pack animals through the rain. But it's exciting to see the steady rate of progress on this island and how far it has reached, at least partially, into the remote rural areas.

THE FUTURE OF THE WORLD'S MOST PERFECT FOOD

If chocolate follows the lead of other farm-to-table-type movements, we're likely to see more locally made, fine-quality chocolate in cities and towns across the nation, and an increased general knowledge of the flavor profiles of various origins and beans. But will this improve the supply chain of the major chocolate corporations? A look at the official position of household names like Hershey's, Nestlé, and Mars—and some recent public commitments—suggests it already has.

Hershey published its first corporate social responsibility report in 2010; today, the company's CSR report sounds a lot like the mission statements of many craft chocolate makers. As of 2017, 75 percent of its cacao was certified by Rainforest Alliance, UTZ, or Fair Trade USA, and the company has made a commitment to source 100 percent of its cacao sustainably by 2020. Hershey supports farmers in their effort to get these certifications, regardless of where their cacao ultimately goes. "They can sell that cacao to whomever they choose. The goal is that they're trained to follow sustainable practices and appropriate labor practices as part of how they're operating their farm," explains Hershey's director of communications, Jeff Beckman.

Hershey also uses the Web app Sourcemap, which provides supply-chain visibility to consumers—at least of some of its products.

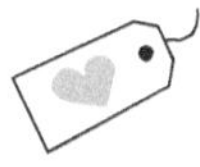

EAT YOUR VALUES

Which bar should you choose? Check out these chocolate visionaries who are focusing on building relationships with farmers, publishing sourcing reports, and changing the world, one bar at a time. As Emily Stone of Uncommon Cacao says, paying a little more can make a real difference to growers. "Look for chocolate bars that are three dollars and up, a good consumer benchmark that farmers have been paid well. If you're willing to spend four or more dollars, you're likely also supporting small-holder farmers and a small business."

Amano: Considered one of the best-tasting bars by many in the craft chocolate industry, Orem, Utah–based Amano chocolate has won gold, silver, and bronze awards for years at the "Olympics of Chocolate"—the International Chocolate Awards—as well as at other competitions. (Yes, there are chocolate competitions.) Founder Art Pollard is obsessed with quality and taste, and has formed direct-trade relationships with farmers in places including Venezuela, Ecuador, the Dominican Republic, and Papua New Guinea. Be sure to try their Raspberry Rose 55%, Madagascar 70%, and Cardamom Black Pepper 60%.

Askinosie: Named one of Forbes's "Best Small Companies in America," this Springfield, Missouri–based family-owned company sells bean-to-bar, single-origin, direct trade chocolate and weaves social responsibility into everything they do, including projects with cooperatives and women's groups in Africa. Askinosie also does profit-sharing with farmers in Ecuador, Tanzania, and the Philippines, and provides lunch to nearly three thousand children at schools in the communities where they work. Each bar has a picture of the farmer on it, which is one way the company tries to connect consumers to the source. Founder Shawn Askinosie is also a Family Brother at Assumption Abbey, a Trappist monastery in Missouri. Try the 60% Dark Chocolate and Peanut Butter from Tanzania (peanut butter sourced from Durham, North Carolina–based Big Spoon Roasters) and Dark Chocolate and Malted Milk 60% bar (malt flavor in collaboration with Jeni's Splendid Ice Creams).

Dandelion Chocolate: This bean-to-bar chocolate factory opened in the Mission District of San Francisco in 2010, partly in homage to formerly SF-based Scharffen Berger. Dandelion takes the art of chocolate very seriously, hand-sorting beans sourced from farmers, painstakingly roasting batches to get the right flavor, and limiting ingredients to cacao and sugar—no added cocoa butter, vanilla, or lecithin. Dandelion is also focused on transparency and consumer education through its website and book. Visit the factory/café in San Francisco or Tokyo and watch chocolate being made while you sip hot chocolate and munch on a pastry. You can also travel with Dandelion to visit cacao producers. Check the website for details. Try bars made from single estates, such as the 70% cacao from Hacienda Azul in Costa Rica.

Endangered Species Chocolate: Using Fairtrade America–certified cacao sourced from West African farmers, Indianapolis, Indiana–based Endangered Species Chocolate donates 10 percent of net profits to support conservation efforts. ESC has a beautiful impact report available online that shows the animals your purchase benefits (rhinos, chimpanzees, and lions, oh my!). You can also see where in the world they live, and how much money the company has given to its wildlife-focused partners—more than $1.3 million in the past three years. Try ESC's Dark Chocolate with Peppermint Crunch 72% and Dark Chocolate with Caramel and Sea Salt 60%.

Guittard: In the mid-1800s, Etienne Guittard left France for California, hoping to strike it rich with gold. He carried chocolate from his uncle's factory to trade for mining supplies. The miners quickly bought up all his chocolate. Recognizing another kind of gold, Guittard sailed back to France to learn the craft, returning to San Francisco in 1868 to open

Guittard Chocolate. Today, this fifth-generation, family-owned company makes fair trade certified bars, chips, and couverture and focuses on community involvement and environmental stewardship.

Pacari: This Ecuadorian company has a direct relationship with its farmers, paying a premium and running social programs. They participate in organic and biodynamic farming and process their own cacao. "It is the best chocolate coming from Latin America that has had the most impact," says chocolate scholar and author Maricel Presilla.

Raaka: This Red Hook, Brooklyn–based chocolate company strives for environmentally and socially responsible production of delicious chocolate creations that showcase "the wilder side of cacao." The certified organic, kosher, non-GMO "wild" bars include flavors such as Bananas Foster (68% cacao, with organic bananas and organic vanilla bean), Coconut Milk (60% cacao) bar from Zorzal Cacao in the Dominican Republic, and the Limited Batch Ginger Snap (70% cacao). You can also book a tour and take a class.

Tabal: Founded in 2012 by former high school principal Dan Bieser, Wauwatosa, Wisconsin–based Tabal is one of the Midwest's few bean-to-bar, certified organic, and kosher chocolate makers, offering, among other things, single-origin bars. Tabal focuses on great chocolate and great relationships, and sources beans from farmers or co-ops in a dozen different locations, including Costa Rica and Colombia. Order online or buy at their chocolate lounge and factory store, where you can also take a class in chocolate. Try their Peru 70% with chili peppers or cherries, and their Dominican Republic Espresso Crunch 70%.

Theo: Founded in Seattle in 2006 by Joe Whinney, Theo is one of the largest and most respected of the bean-to-bar makers, and a pioneer organic cacao user. Whinney reportedly fell in love with Central America and Africa in the late 1990s and formed a chocolate company to share the love. Theo has relationships with individual farmers and cooperatives, and pays far above the commodity price. Take a factory tour at the Seattle location to learn more. Try the Coconut Turmeric Chocolate Clusters, Salted Almond 70% Dark Chocolate, and Cinnamon Horchata 45% Milk Chocolate bar.

Together We Bake: Not a craft chocolate maker, this Alexandria, Virginia–based nonprofit helps women who have left abusive homes, overcome addiction, or transitioned out of prison by giving them a second chance. Together We Bake employs women, teaching them to make delicious chocolate chip cookies according to a secret recipe. I love these cookies, and I bring them to every To the Market event possible to highlight their great work (and have great snacks on hand).

Valrhona: Valrhona has been making chocolate in the small village of Tain-l'Hermitage, France, since 1922. Until the craft chocolate movement began, Valrhona was considered the best chocolate in the world—for both eating and baking—by many chocoholics and professional pastry chefs. Despite its size, Valrhona is also considered a bean-to-bar maker by some. The company has even begun operating its own plantations in Venezuela and the Dominican Republic. Valrhona is also a leader in social programs at the source, fostering good relationships with farmers and paying attention to detail from bean to bar.

And one more thing . . . You can help preserve high-quality cacao and the livelihood of those who farm it by donating to the Heirloom Cacao Preservation Fund (HCPF). This nonprofit, launched in 2012 in partnership with the U.S. Department of Agriculture and the Fine Chocolate Industry Association, is dedicated to protecting cacao diversity and improving the lives of farmers who grow fine-quality heirloom cacao species. The HCPF helps cacao farmers deal with environmental change, deforestation, and economic influences threatening these distinctive, high-quality cacao trees. The HCPF is the first initiative to identify and map high-quality, endangered cacao and certify growers.

You can trace the source of certain ingredients in Hershey's Milk Chocolate Bars with Almonds and Reese's Peanut Butter Cups using this online tool. I think this is a great start. Hershey also continues to source from small farms like Finca Elvesia in the D.R. for Scharffen Berger and Dagoba, and having the might of a major corporation behind them is benefiting these specialty lines.

In 2017, Dagoba's new brand manager, a former social worker turned chocolate evangelist named Susie Picken Burch, convinced Target to carry four new bars from Dagoba in all 1,800 of its U.S. stores. This was a huge order for this small company, and one that translated into more beans being bought from Finca Elvesia and other small farms. Burch is also developing programs to help increase women's agency in the four countries of origin that supply cacao to Dagoba, starting with Peru.

Closer to home, Hershey is helping stock a food pantry for schoolkids and their families in the Derry Township school district of Pennsylvania, where the company's headquarters are and where food insecurity is a problem for some.

The Hershey Company is also part of the industry group World Cocoa Foundation (WCF), as are the other major brands. Through WCF, the big chocolate companies have founded something called CocoaAction, an industry-wide strategy focused on sustainability. In 2016, these major producers also joined another WCF initiative, the Climate Smart Cocoa Program, which aims to strengthen public/private partnerships to address the threat of climate change on the cacao supply. (Kellogg's, owner of a Girl Scout bakery, is also participating in this program, which I was so happy to discover.) "We started talking about the problems we're facing, and openly sharing information as much as possible about the farmer," says Jeff King, senior director of sustainability, CSR, and social innovation at Hershey. "The industry

DASH ON DOWN TO THE DOMINICAN REPUBLIC

The D.R. has become an incredibly popular beach destination, but to see the agricultural economy at work, head inland and upland to tour a cacao farm.

Tour: Cacao Chocolate Tours, guided by team members from Rizek Cacao, bring you to La Esmeralda, where you can follow the cacao journey, from planting to processing. Or go with one of the island's many tour operators to visit a farm affiliated with Conacado, the D.R.'s national confederation of cacao producers, to taste raw cacao and hot chocolate.

Walk: The capital city of Santo Domingo is a late-night kind of place. The time zone is an hour later than the East Coast, and that fact, combined with the Latin culture, means restaurants and clubs don't get going until eight or nine or ten, and you'll hear merengue music blasting until well past midnight. Stroll down the pedestrian Calle el Conde in the amazingly preserved, super clean, pedestrian-friendly Colonial Zone, a waterfront enclave of sixteenth-century homes, churches, historic sites, boutiques, restaurants, and hotels.

Shop: Artists set up their wares right on the Calle el Conde, bright paintings of island life, carvings, weavings, and more. Also in Santo Domingo, check out Kah Kow, a charming chocolate boutique with two locations, owned by Rizek, that sells chocolate bars made on the island from local cacao, as well as hot chocolate, T-shirts, soap, prints of famous local buildings done in a beautiful impressionistic style, and an adorable stuffed cacao pod toy called Poddy. You can also sign up for a fifteen-minute make-your-own-chocolate session.

Eat: In Santo Domingo, you can find Dominican food at various restaurants. For something lighter, check out Time Vegetarian Kitchen in the Colonial Zone, which bakes olive oil rolls to order and makes huge "pizzas"—crisp shells with Caesar salad on top.

Stay: Hodelpa Nicolas Ovando is an incredibly romantic hotel in the Colonial Zone that is listed as a World Heritage Site by UNESCO. Rooms are in three stone houses built in 1502, which are connected by patios and walkways and include the original home of the town's founder, Governor Nicolás de Ovando. It's a popular local spot for weddings that go late into the night; if merengue music in the courtyard will keep you up, drop by for drinks or dinner rather than checking in.

is extremely proud of the fact that they were able to come together and meet around the table and talk about these issues."

Nestlé is focusing on reducing labor exploitation, particularly of children, in the supply chain through its Child Labour Monitoring and Remediation System. This program is part of Nestlé's 2030 goal to help improve the livelihoods of thirty million people in communities directly connected to its business activities. Nestlé UK also released a report in response to the UK Modern Slavery Act, detailing its efforts to fight both adult and child exploitation in its chocolate supply chain, as well as in its other categories, like fishing.

Nestlé is also focusing on women's economic empowerment in the cacao industry and in its own leadership, which I find particularly heartening. The company has partnered with the Fair Labor Association to boost women's roles in Côte d'Ivoire, for example, and to offer training in new skills to diversify income in Ecuador and Venezuela.

According to Nestlé CSR reports, in 2016 the company helped more than one thousand women develop income-generating side activities in Côte d'Ivoire.

Mars, a privately owned, $35 billion corporation that sells M&M'S, Snickers, Twix, and Dove, among other chocolate-based treats, has pledged $1 billion toward its own cacao sustainability efforts. Called Sustainable in a Generation, this climate-action initiative aims to reduce the company's carbon footprint—including that of suppliers—by more than 60 percent by 2050, and to entirely eliminate greenhouse gas emissions from its direct operations by 2040. Sustainable in a Generation also focuses on water stewardship, land management, and improving the lives of the million or so people in the Mars supply chain.

As Barry Parkin, Mars's chief sustainability officer, recently said, "There are obviously commitments the world is leaning into but, frankly, we don't think we're getting there fast enough collectively." Mars is also working with the Innovative Genomics Institute, a research lab at the University of California, Berkeley, to develop a cacao hybrid that can withstand climate change.

In 2017, the nonprofit environmental advocacy and action group Mighty Earth launched an extensive investigation into cacao farming in Ghana and Côte d'Ivoire and released a report revealing the negative environmental impact. Following this campaign—and international media coverage of it—twenty-four of the world's leading cocoa companies signed a pact to end deforestation in the region. Godiva, for example, promised to roll out a cross-commodity zero-deforestation policy, including in cacao. In February 2018, Hershey announced its commitment to buying 100 percent zero-deforestation cacao, effective immediately.

As a lifelong lover of all these established brands, I find the move toward supply-chain transparency in Big Chocolate particularly

MADE IN HAWAII: THE UNITED STATES GETS IN ON CACAO FARMING

Like coffee in California, cacao can also be grown in the United States. This is the vision of Dylan Butterbaugh, the young owner of Manoa Chocolate Hawaii, a bean-to-bar chocolate company that began in 2010.

Growing up in Hawaii, Butterbaugh was obsessed with surfing. He traveled the world in search of the world's best waves. In college, he double-majored in sustainable development and Spanish, but was still more focused on surfing than on much else.

In his senior year, he started to think about his future and what he might want to do with his degree. He met someone at the university who was studying cacao as a potential agricultural product to grow in Hawaii. Butterbaugh was excited by the idea of supporting Hawaiian agriculture through a product that brings so much happiness. He started watching YouTube videos about the chocolate-making process and experimenting with making it at home. He and his friends rigged chocolate-making equipment from household items, and recorded their efforts in some pretty hilarious videos. You can see him roasting cacao beans over a gas barbecue grill in his parents' yard, and working a pedal-powered winnowing machine made from a bicycle and a back massager. "We built everything for hundreds of dollars," he says.

Butterbaugh looks like a young tech-preneur crossed with a surfer. He wears his thick, brown hair cut short and parted on the side, and moves with a bouncy, energetic, athletic gait. He has a youthful voice and an enthusiasm that makes you want to buy his bars.

Like me, his chocolate-eating background was mostly Hershey's milk chocolate. Unlike me, he didn't love it. But while learning about the field, he discovered craft dark chocolate and became hooked.

He started his first factory with a $15,000 bank loan and a Kickstarter campaign that generated $19,000 more. Manoa officially opened in 2012. It's a great example of how possible it is today for someone with no real experience to get into this industry and make a difference while doing so.

Today, Manoa has twenty-one employees and operates a factory, tasting room, and retail store in Oahu, and a second retail store in the Hyatt hotel in Waikiki. Manoa sources from Hawaii as well as from other countries, and makes single-origin bars and "inclusion bars," with ingredients such as sea salt, lavender, coffee, and cocoa nibs.

Because the labor and land costs are so high in Hawaii, local beans are very expensive. Manoa pays the high price or gets cacao beans from farmers, makes chocolate with them, and then pays the farmers through profits from the bars. This revenue share model generates three to four times more income for farmers than selling raw beans.

Butterbaugh's main passion today is continuing to build a new industry in his home state. "I love what it can become. That you can take a fruit tree that grows here, make a high-end, value-added product, and export it all over the world. The bigger we get, the more fruit trees get planted."

The sugar industry in Hawaii has really dried up, and Butterbaugh sees chocolate as the island's next big crop. "I compare it to Napa Valley, which is also really expensive, but is covered in grapevines because they're selling wine, not grapes. We can add value to the crop and create a finished chocolate bar, which makes the process work here." He also looks to wine as a model in terms of respecting the varietal and terroir. His vision is to create a market for Hawaiian beans as a specific flavor, and then market the bars as the first made-*and-grown*-in-America chocolate. "We're obsessed with making excellent chocolate in an ethical way."

sweet. As King puts it, "Business is one of the gateways to solving larger social issues, partly because of the perpetual funding. If you know a product you are buying is supporting a program you care about, you know money is flowing in for that issue. The consumer world is changing. Transparency is becoming ubiquitous. All companies are learning to give the consumer what they want and deserve."

For us as consumers, we can help in so many ways (such as by eating more chocolate) and by continuing to ask how our products are being made. Whether we choose to make our impact through chocolate, or coffee, or artisan enterprise, we all have a part in building great industries, and helping rebuild the ones we love.

Of course, just as the problems of the world can seem overwhelming, so can attempting to change every single thing you buy. None of us can do everything. If you can find one area to work on through your purchasing power, you are part of the solution. I'm so excited to watch as the benefits for all of us unfold.

ACKNOWLEDGMENTS

I want to first start by thanking the team that has helped make this book a reality. I am deeply grateful to Wendy Paris for collaborating with me on this journey and to Leigh Flayton for identifying Wendy as a strong partner for this project. Wendy's extraordinary talent for crafting a compelling narrative inspired me and made the research and writing process exciting. I am thankful for her friendship and leadership throughout the book's development. I also want to thank my editors for their support. When I met Sara Carder, I was certain she shared my vision for the book and immediately connected with her passion for social change. Similarly, a huge thanks to Joanna Ng for her insightful feedback on the manuscript. I am over the moon to be a part of the Penguin Random House family and couldn't imagine a better home for this book than TarcherPerigee. I also want to thank my literary agent, Kirsten Neuhaus of Foundry, for believing in this project and taking on a new author. I look forward to many more projects together. Finally, to Ann Sardini and Anna Worrall for planting the seed that I should write this book.

Outside of my book collaborators, I have many people to thank for so much unconditional love. I am a product of an extraordinary support network and want to attempt to acknowledge, albeit inadequately, what others have given to me.

I owe an enormous debt of gratitude to my best friend and husband, Nate. He has tolerated my building a venture-backed business while writing a book without ever complaining about my challenging schedule. He has steadfastly supported me at each stage of the writing process and his work ethic and vision for his own career have inspired me to think and do even bigger things with my life than I ever thought possible. I am in constant awe of everything he has created and can't imagine spending my time on this planet with anyone else.

Similarly, I cannot express sufficient appreciation to my loving parents, Catherine and Rob. They modeled for me a life of service to others and taught me how to love and value everyone. They also instilled in me the confidence to unapologetically be myself and to pay little, if any, attention to what others thought of me. They also modeled how to live their faith and I am grateful to them for helping me be deeply grounded in my beliefs. I also so appreciate my broader family, including my hilarious and exceptionally bright siblings, Peter and Meredith. I feel so lucky to have grown up in a household with so much laughter and kindness. Similarly, my extended family, especially my fabulous godmother and aunt, Kathi, my cousin/little brother, Bayly, and my second cousin/business champion, Clint. Thank you to my grandparents, Marion, Ray, Bob, and my namesake, Jane.

I also want to thank my dearest friends for helping support me throughout my career and for offering nothing but endless encouragement at each stage. This includes, but is in no way limited to, Annie, Becky, Jamie, Jen, Jessica, Kelly, Kirsty, LeAnne, Leyla, Lindsey, Liz, Maggie, and Rachel. Thank you for always asking how you can help make my dreams a reality and never demonstrating anything but loyalty and love. I am also grateful for my colleagues from my days at the Office of Counterterrorism (particularly my Regional's crew!), the Office of Global Women's Issues, and the McCain Institute. Each community helped me grow and I know how fortunate I am to have developed such deep friendships in each location.

I was blessed with extraordinary teachers throughout my schooling as well, especially Zach Goodyear, Leigh Dingwall, and Sylvia Bartz.

Last, I want to give thanks for every single person who has helped build To the Market. Without the leap of faith that To the Market's team, advisory board members, investors, the Target + Techstars community, clients, and suppliers took by partnering with me, To the Market would not be what it has become today. In particular, I want to extend my deep gratitude to the heroic To the Market team, especially Jill and Danielle. Thank you for working nights, weekends, and even through vacations to build a thriving business and make positive change in the world. Your belief in me means more than I can ever articulate.

—Jane Mosbacher Morris

I am so grateful to Jane Mosbacher Morris for inviting me to be part of this book. It's been an incredibly educational, uplifting, and deeply satisfying project that has taught me a great deal about looking behind systemic problems to see root causes, the worlds of fashion and retail, and the role business can play in economic and social development. It also gave me a chance to see, firsthand, how coffee and chocolate are grown and produced, something I'd never witnessed, despite my total dependence on and abiding love for these two staples. Thanks to Alejandro Keller, vice president of AnaCafé, and Arnoldo Melgar, executive director of Funcafé, for help meeting some of Guatemala's best coffee growers, and Rob Everts at Equal Exchange. Thanks also to everyone who helped with coffee background, including: Greg D'Alesandre of Dandelion Chocolate; Kim Elena Ionescu, chief sustainability officer at the Specialty Coffee Association; Raina Lang and Jenny Parker McCloskey at Conservation International; Peter Longo, owner of Porto Rico Importing Company; Joan Harper of Fair Trade LA; and Carol at Kishe Coffee.

Callie Murphy, Annie Holschuh, and Bridget Tishler at BVK and the Dominican Republic Ministry of Tourism provided assistance in the Dominican Republic. Thanks also to those who helped on-island and on background, including José Locandro of Risek, Jaime Gomez of Conocado, and Bernardo Padilla; Finca Elvesia's Isidro Castillo, and Emily Stone of Uncommon Cacao.

I had a lot of support during what was a very compressed writing schedule. Thanks to my cousins Mark and Shari Sokol for being my Atlanta family and putting me up during the final writing deadline week. Thanks to Laura Rich for keeping me company at the Miami Airport, which seemed briefly my second home. Thanks to my mom, Joy Paris, for babysitting while I was in Guatemala, and to my son, Alexander Paris-Callahan, for being a consummate good sport about having a writer for a mother and enthusiastically doing "late nights" along with me.

—Wendy Paris

SELECTED READING

We consulted a variety of books while writing this one. Here are some great things to read.

Danticat, Edwidge. *After the Dance: A Walk Through Carnival in Jacmel, Haiti*, reprint edition (Vintage, 2015).

Giller, Megan. *Bean-to-Bar Chocolate: America's Craft Chocolate Revolution: The Origins, the Makers, and the Mind-Blowing Flavors* (Storey Publishing, 2017).

Masonis, Todd, Greg D'Alesandre, Lisa Vega, and Molly Gore. *Making Chocolate: From Bean to Bar to S'More* (Potter, 2017).

Menchú, Rigoberta. *I, Rigoberta Menchú: An Indian Woman in Guatemala*, 2nd edition. Edited by Elisabeth Burgos-Debray, translated by Ann Wright (Verso, 2010).

Presilla, Maricel E. *The New Taste of Chocolate: A Cultural and Natural History of Cacao with Recipes* (Ten Speed Press, 2009).

Savitz, Andrew. *The Triple Bottom Line: How Today's Best-Run Companies Are Achieving Economic, Social and Environmental Success—and How You Can Too*, 2nd edition (Jossey-Bass, 2013).

NOTES

INTRODUCTION

Page 5. **The average American family earns nearly $75,000 a year . . .** Esther Bloom, "See How Your Spending Compares with That of the Average American—and the U.S. Government," CNBC.com, September 27, 2017.

Page 5. **International trade in artisan-made products, what the United Nations calls "art and crafts," generates about $32 billion each year.** United Nations, *Creative Economy Report,* 2010.

Page 17. **Retail is a massive force in the U.S. economy—a $2.6 trillion industry, two-thirds of our total gross domestic product (GDP).** National Retail Federation/PricewaterhouseCoopers, "The Economic Impact of the U.S. Retail Industry," September 2014.

CHAPTER ONE: WEAR YOUR VALUES

Page 26. **The International Labour Organization estimates that human trafficking is a $150 billion industry . . .** U.S. Department of State, "Trafficking in Persons Report," June 2017.

Page 26. **Sexual exploitation has devastating consequences . . .** M. Abas, et al., "Risk Factors for Mental Disorders in Women Survivors of Human Trafficking: a Historical Cohort Study," *BMC Psychiatry* 13 (August 2013): 204–14.

Page 30. **Greek coins often had the first one or two letters . . .** Raquel Laneri, "Is Monogramming Classy or Tacky?" *Forbes* (November 30, 2010).

Page 30. **One popular way to assert status was by monogramming linens . . .** W. B. Carpenter, "Monograms," *Appletons' Journal* 5, no. 108 (April 22, 1871): 464–466.

Page 31. **(I read a hilarious op-ed by the investor Lawrence Lenihan . . .** Lawrence Lenihan, "Op-Ed: How Small Will Beat Big and Save the Fashion Industry," *Business of Fashion*, June 19, 2017.

Page 34. **Recent Pew research on millennials found that members of this generation . . .** "Millennials in Adulthood: Detached from Institutions, Networked with Friends," Pew Research Center, March 7, 2014.

Page 34. **In 2015, more than 80 percent of Fortune 500 companies published CSR reports . . .** "Flash Report: 81% of S&P 500 Companies Published Sustainability Reports in 2015," Governance and Accountability Institute, March 15, 2016.

Page 40. **As the state's resource guide on the act puts it, "An estimated 21 million people—11.4 million women and girls . . .** Kamala D. Harris, California Department of Justice, "The California Transparency in Supply Chains Act: A Resource Guide," 2015.

Page 41. **. . . as a recent survey of Western consumers . . .** "Does It Pay to Be Good?" *Sloan Management Review*, winter 2009.

Page 41. **In Europe, the United Kingdom's Modern Slavery Act of 2015 is designed to tackle slavery . . .** "Modern Slavery Act 2015," http://www.legislation.gov.uk/ukpga/2015/30/contents/enacted.

CHAPTER TWO: THIS BRACELET BUILDS COMMUNITY

Page 56. **The average American spends almost $1,000 a year on holiday presents . . .** Amanda Haury, "Average Cost of an American Christmas," Investopedia.com, December 20, 2017.

Page 57. **As Harvard psychologist Ellen J. Langer has noted, refusing a present prevents someone else from experiencing the joy of giving.** Tara Parker-Pope, "The Gift That Gives Right Back? The Giving Itself," *The New York Times*, December 11, 2007.

Page 58. **The gift market is an estimated $130 billion plus each year . . .** Tom Popomaronis, "This $22 Billion Industry Is Dying. Meet the Startup Reviving It," *Inc.*, November 14, 2016.

Page 65. **This desire to sell something different has spurred the growth of private label clothing . . .** Matthew Boyle, "The Retail Apocalypse Is Fueled by No-Name Clothes," Bloomberg.com, December 12, 2017.

Page 67. **By the 1700s, the Europeans were calling Haiti the "Jewel of the Antilles" . . .** Bob Corbett, "Why Is Haiti So Poor?" Faculty.Webster.Edu, 1986.

Page 67. **Today, Haiti is the poorest nation in the Western hemisphere.** Jon Lee Anderson, "Haiti Has a President," *The New Yorker*, February 17, 2016.

Page 68. **Then Secretary of State Hillary Clinton is reported to have responded . . .** Jon Lee Anderson, "Letter from Haiti," *The New Yorker*, February 1, 2016.

Page 68. **As *New Yorker* writer Jon Lee Anderson put it in a 2016 article . . .** Ibid.

Page 69. **Though the Clinton Bush Haiti Fund has closed down . . .** Telephone interview, Nathalie Tancrede, January 18, 2017.

Page 77. **Christopher Columbus was apparently impressed by the woodwork and weaving of the Arawak . . .** Eleanor Ingalls Christensen, *The Art of Haiti* (A.S. Barnes, 1975).

Page 82. **More than a quarter of Americans spend eighty dollars or more on a birthday present for their significant other.** "How Much Do You Spend on Birthday Gifts?" Proflowers, com, July 13, 2015.

CHAPTER THREE: YOUR LATTE CAN IMPROVE LIVES

Page 90. **But globally, we consume something like six hundred billion cups of coffee a year . . .** Guy Pearse, *The Greenwash Effect: Corporate Deception, Celebrity Environmentalists, and What Big Business Isn't Telling You About Their Products and Brands* (Skyhorse Publishing, 2014).

Page 90. **More than 25 million smallholder farmers grow coffee . . .** http://www.rainforest-alliance.org/articles/rainforest-alliance-certified-coffee; Lora Jones, "Coffee: Who Grows, Drinks and Pays the Most?" BBC News, April 13, 2018.

Page 90. In one study published in the *Archives of Internal Medicine*, women who drank four or more cups of coffee a day . . . Michel Lucas, et al., "Coffee, Caffeine, and Risk of Depression Among Women," *Archives of Internal Medicine* (September 26, 2011): 1571–78, doi: 10.1001/archinternmed.2011.393.

Page 90. In the United States, we spend $40 billion . . . https://www.hsph.harvard.edu/news/multimedia-article/facts/.

Page 93. As Bambi Semroc of Conservation International explains, resentment can build . . . Telephone interview with Bambi Semroc, September 13, 2017.

Page 99. This fungus, which has been attacking the leaves of coffee trees since the late nineteenth century . . . Jesse Bladyka, "Coffee Leaf Rust: A New Reality for Specialty Coffee," Specialty Coffee Association News, April 11, 2015.

CHAPTER 4: WHY REINVENT THE WHEEL WHEN YOU CAN REPURPOSE IT?

Page 134. Even back then, in ancient Rome, Julius Caesar had to confront removal and recycling of . . . Martin Medina, "Scavenging in Historical Perspective," *The World's Scavengers: Salvaging for Sustainable Production* (Lanham, MD: AltaMira, 2007), 18–21.

Page 134. Companies today are increasingly setting zero waste goals . . . Mary Mazzoni, "3p Weekend: 10 Companies Going Zero Waste to Landfill," TriplePundit, January 6, 2017.

Page 138. Methane gas traps heat in the atmosphere even more than carbon dioxide does. Gayathri Vaidyanathan, "How Bad of a Greenhouse Gas Is Methane?" *Scientific American*, December 22, 2015.

Page 138. We create at least 3.5 million tons of solid waste a day . . . Kadir van Lohuizen Noor, *The Washington Post*, November 21, 2017.

Page 145. Globally, we've produced about 83 million metric tons of plastic, and less than 10 percent gets recycled. Roland Geyer et al., "Production, Use, and Fate of All Plastics Ever Made," *Science Advances* 3, no. 7 (July 5, 2017).

Page 147. **It can take one thousand years for a plastic bag to degrade.** "Tips to Use Less Plastic," Green Education Foundation, 2017.

Page 153. **"They'd come to the orphanage to visit their children," she says.** Telephone interview with Shelly Jean, August 23, 2017.

Page 156. **As Callie Himsl, an American who works at Papillon, puts it . . .** Telephone interview with Callie Himsl, July 4, 2017.

Page 165. **Atlanta's football team, the Falcons, recently did an amazing partnership with Novelis . . .** Gracie Bonds Staples, "How Many Aluminum Cans Does It Take to Build a Home?" *Atlanta Journal-Constitution*, July 20, 2017.

Page 165. **American businesses toss about one million toner cartridges every single day . . .** Scott Bowen, "Taking Them Back: How Recycling Toner Containers Helps the Planet," *Forbes*, August 10, 2017.

CHAPTER FIVE: NOT ALL FACTORIES ARE EQUAL, OR EVIL

Page 171. **Between the years 2000 and 2014, the number of garments . . .** Nathalie Remy, Eveline Speelman, and Steven Swartz, "Style That's Sustainable: A New Fast-Fashion Formula," McKinsey.com, October 2016.

Page 171. **The most infamous accident in a U.S. sweatshop occurred at the Triangle Shirtwaist Company factory in New York City . . .** Hadassa Kosak, "Triangle Shirtwaist Fire," *Jewish Women's Archive Encyclopedia*, jwa.org; "Complete Transcript of Triangle Fire," November 20, 1911, available through Cornell University ILR School, Kheel Center for Labor-Management Documentation & Archives, Digital Archives; "Don't Mourn—Organize: Lessons from the Triangle Shirtwaist Factory Fire," New York Committee for Occupational Safety and Health, March 25, 2011.

Page 173. **. . . American factories began ramping up production . . .** "Mass Production," *Encyclopedia.com.*; A. J. Baime, "How Detroit Won World War II," History.com.

Page 174. **As Oren Shaffer, then chief financial officer at the Goodyear Tire and Rubber Company, told the *New York Times* in 1989 . . .** Louis Uchitelle, "Spread of U.S. Plants Abroad Is Slowing Exports," *The New York Times*, March 26, 1989.

Page 174. But U.S. companies also began doing something else that troubled . . . Constantinos C. Markides and Norman Berg, "Manufacturing Offshore Is Bad for Business," *Harvard Business Review*, September 1988.

Page 178. Buyers can put serious pressure on factory owners and managers . . . Sidney Leng, "Can Chinese Manufacturers Ever Be Clean, Green and Profitable? Garment Factories Search for the Answer," *South China Morning Post*, September 12, 2017.

Page 179. According to a United Nations 2017 World Water Development Report, more than 80 percent of the world's wastewater . . . "Wastewater: The Untapped Resource," United Nations World Water Development Report, 2017.

Page 179. In the United States, some companies have moved away from environmentally harmful production practices . . . Yue Maggie Zhou, "When Some US Firms Move Production Overseas, They Also Offshore Their Pollution," *The Conversation*, May 18, 2017.

Page 179. As sustainable fashion pioneer Eileen Fisher has put it . . . Nancy Szokan, "The Fashion Industry Tries to Take Responsibility for Its Pollution," *The Washington Post*, June 30, 2016.

Page 180. This was the worst garment factory disaster in known history. Dominic Rushe, "Retail Group Approves Bangladesh Factories as Safety Concerns Persist, Report Finds," *The Guardian*, November 21, 2016.

Page 181. After the Rana Plaza disaster in Bangladesh, many fashion industry leaders . . . Ibid.

CHAPTER SIX: JUST DESSERTS FOR EVERYONE

Page 205. The average cacao farmer in Ghana makes eighty-four cents a day, while farmers in Côte d'Ivoire earn about fifty cents a day. Etelle Higonnet, Marisa Bellantonio, Glenn Hurowitz, "Chocolate's Dark Secret: How the Cocoa Industry Destroys National Parks," *Mighty Earth*, 2017.

Page 205. Chocolate is part of the livelihood of some estimated fifty million people worldwide, more than five million of whom are smallholder cocoa farmers. World Cocoa Foundation, "About Cocoa."

Page 207. Many leading small-scale chocolate makers watched videos about making chocolate at home on the website Chocolate Alchemy . . . Kim

Severson, "The Kitchen-Counter Chocolatiers," *New York Times*, February 10, 2015.

Page 212. **Dark chocolate lovers so often look down on milk chocolate . . .** Julia Moskin, "Dark May Be King, But Milk Chocolate Makes a Move," *The New York Times*, February 13, 2008.

Page 226. **"They can sell that cacao to whomever they choose. The goal is that they're trained to follow sustainable practices and appropriate labor . . ."** Telephone interview with Jeff Beckman, January 4, 2018.

Page 231. **"We started talking about the problems we're facing, and openly sharing information as much as possible about the farmer . . ."** Telephone interview with Jeff King, January 4, 2018.

Page 234. **As Barry Parkin, Mars's chief sustainability officer, recently said, "There are obviously commitments . . ."** Erin Brodwin, "Chocolate Is on Track to Go Extinct in 40 Years," *Business Insider*, December 31, 2017.

Page 234. **In 2017, the nonprofit environmental advocacy and action group Mighty Earth launched an extensive investigation into cacao farming in Ghana and Côte d'Ivoire and released a report revealing the negative environmental impact.** Wendy Paris, "A Mighty Grant: With Modest Support, This Environmental Group Achieved Big Changes," *Inside Philanthropy*, March 23, 2018.

INDEX

ABOUT THE AUTHORS

(Kristen Loken)

Jane Mosbacher Morris is the founder and CEO of To the Market, which connects businesses and consumers to ethically made products from around the world. She previously served as the director of humanitarian action for the McCain Institute for International Leadership, where she managed the institute's anti–human trafficking program, and currently serves on the institute's Human Trafficking Advisory Council. Earlier, she worked in the U.S. Department of State's Bureau of Counterterrorism and in the Secretary's Office of Global Women's Issues. Morris is a member of VF Corporation's Advisory Council on Responsible Sourcing. She holds a bachelor of science in foreign service from Georgetown University and a master of business administration degree from Columbia Business School. She is a term member at the Council on Foreign Relations and sits on the advisory board of Speak Your Silence. She is married to Nate Morris of Kentucky.

(Sonia Sones)

Wendy Paris is an author and journalist who has written about arts and culture, travel, business, and psychology for a variety of publications, including the *New York Times*, *Psychology Today*, Salon.com, *Los Angeles Review of Books*, InsidePhilanthropy.com, *Jewish Journal*, *ArtNews*, *Travel & Leisure*, and *Condé Nast Traveler*. She loves to collaborate with business and thought leaders to turn good ideas into inspiring, empowering books. She has an MFA in creative nonfiction writing from Columbia University and was a 2012 Fellow with the Encore Foundation and a 2013 Fellow with the New America Foundation. Her last book was *Splitopia: Dispatches from Today's Good Divorce and How to Part Well* (Atria/Simon & Schuster, 2016). Paris is a mentor-editor with the Op-Ed Project. This is her fourth book. She lives in Santa Monica, California, with her son, Alexander, and their dog, Marshmallow.

Penguin Random House LLC
1745 Broadway
US-NY, 10019
US
https://www.penguinrandomhouse.com
1-800-733-3000

The authorized representative in the EU for product safety and compliance is

Penguin Random House Ireland
Morrison Chambers, 32 Nassau Street
D02 YH68
IE
https://eu-contact.penguin.ie

ISBN: 9798217185924
Release ID: 155245421

www.ingramcontent.com/pod-product-compliance
Lightning Source LLC
LaVergne TN
LVHW100521110826
845146LV00002B/730
* 9 7 9 8 2 1 7 1 8 5 9 2 4 *